CLASSIC SPEEDBOATS
1916-1939

——■——

For Isabelle.

This edition published in 1997 by Motorbooks International
Publishers and Wholesalers, 729 Prospect Avenue, PO Box 1, Osceola, WI
54020-0001 USA

Graphic Design : Isabelle Cransac

First published in French by E.T.A.I. by Boulogne-Billancourt, France in 1995
© Copyright E.T.A.I., Paris 1995
English translation © Copyright Motorbooks International, Inc., 1997

ISBN 0-7603-0464-5

Front Cover: The original *Arab IV* was a 1916 stepped-hull hydroplane which,
although initially successful, sank during a race in 1920. This replica gets its
power from a 500hp Chevrolet V8 engine—similar output compared to the
original V12 Aero engine.

Back cover, top: The *Miss Columbia*, left, is a replica of the original 1924
boat and is powered by 250hp Packard Gold Cup engine. *Baby Bootlegger*
was built of Honduras mahogany with an oak keel by the Nevins boatyard
of City Island, New York.

Back cover, center: *Its a Wonder* is a good example of the new style that
became popular in the 1930s. The "three-point hulls" yielded competitive
speeds even when equipped with older power plants.

Back Cover, bottom: The *Miss Daytona* has been refurbished and fitted
with a Miller engine, as was the original boat.

Printed in Spain

CLASSIC SPEEDBOATS
1916-1939

Gérald Guétat

with Éric Ledru

Translated by James Taylor

Motorbooks International
Publishers & Wholesalers ®

ACKNOWLEDGMENTS

■

This book could not have been written without the friendship and help of a large number of historic speedboat enthusiasts in France, in the United States, in Britain and in Italy. And these acknowledgments must begin with a mention of the enthusiastic contribution and the knowledge of Kenney B. Bassett. Right from the start of the project, he has been a faithful friend and a guide who steered me towards all the preserved American boats which are mentioned in this book.

Those people listed below have provided invaluable help by their support, their advice and their knowledge, as well as through the many rare documents and photographs they have willingly made available to me. My sincere gratitude goes to all of them:

The Antique and Classic Boat Society, its members and organizers; William Borel; Griffith Borgeson; Jean-Paul Caron; John Clark; Gérard Crombac; Richard Crump; Bill Danforth; Kevin Desmond; Alec Giaimo; Deborah M. Di Gregorio; John Hewett; Jean Houët; Rupert Marks; Mark P. Mason; José Mawet; Kenneth M. Muscatel; Elizabeth Parker-Rafferty; Henry-Jacques Pechdimaldjian; Jacques Potherat; Jim Price; Philip Sharples; Victoria Sharps; Everett Smith; Marc Tienda; Eric Vargiolu; Peter Vermilya; The Antique Boat Museum (Clayton, New York); The Mariners Museum, Newport News (Virginia); The Mystic Museum, Seaport (Connecticut) ; and The Unlimited Hall of Fame, Seattle (Washington).

The owners of the preserved boats featured in this book deserve a special word of thanks for their patience and their kindness. Without their dedicated labors, it would sadly no longer be possible to see these witnesses to an exciting past on the water today: John Binley, Michael Bowman, David Coffin, Robert Cox, Richard Crump, Gerald Davidson, Charles Davis, John Eidt, Joseph Fleming, Bud Finkl, Joseph Frauenheim, Thomas Frauenheim, John Hewett, George Hicks, Mark Howard, Joseph Keefe, George Kreissle, Peter Kreissle, (the late) Edward Larter, Adrien Maeght, Barbara Magnuson, Geoffrey Magnuson, Rupert Marks, Mark Mason, Harold Mistele, Wayne Mocksfield, William Morgan, Larry Mullins, Bill Munro, Barb and Cap Peckham, Don Price, Arnold Rubinstein, Chuck Schwager, Mario Scopinich, Philip Sharples, Ray Tischer, Murray Walker, The Basildon Museum (GB), The Antique Boat Museum (Clayton, New York), The Conservatoire international de la plaisance (Bordeaux), The Mercedes-Benz Museum (Stuttgart), and The State of Pennsylvania.

I should also express my thanks to all those enthusiastic and selfless individuals who organize events for preserved speedboats all over the world, as well as to those who restore, maintain and lovingly preserve these historical treasures for future generations.

CONTENTS

FOREWORD

It all began a few years ago on a deserted road in New Hampshire, in the north-eastern United States. Following up some classified advertisements, I was on the trail of a number of old boats and, tired after my journey from France, I was wondering how much further to go. I had three addresses, but there was time to visit only one of them before nightfall. Having lost my way, I pushed open the door of an old railway shed which had fallen on hard times and there, in the half-darkness, I discovered a mahogany hull, long, gleaming and set off by some chromework. The man who was working alone around this splendid object was amazed to learn the nationality of his visitor. A friendship grew from this unexpected encounter, and I was steered from surprise to surprise and given the chance to explore areas where the very rarest of racing boats were to be found.

It was then that the project of bringing back to life the exploits of the pioneer speedboat racers took shape. The subject is so vast that I had to establish certain limits. So this is not a general history of speedboats—far from it, as it focuses on competition. Nor does it include the story of those boats powered by outboard motors; their adventures have been evolving at the forefront of technology since the 1920s and deserve a book to themselves. What this book contains is the story of speedboats with inboard engines, the runabouts which evolved between 1916 and 1939.

The story begins during the First World War, which was a decisive technical turning-point when aero engines became prominent and the United States became the leading world power. This first phase of the story finishes in 1939, with the picture of a fast patrol boat whose hull and engines had been directly developed from 23 years of top-class competition. Huge strides had been made thanks to the hard work of the engineers and the daring of the pilots: the world record had risen from 60mph to 120mph, as car and aircraft technology had steadily advanced. My text provides a historical overview, punctuated by striking facts, anecdotes and quotations which reflect the atmosphere of the times. With the advantage of two generations' hindsight, it was tempting also to take a new perspective on the era of the great heroes of speed.

I was also tempted to draw a parallel between archive and current pictures of boats which were significant in their time, in order to create a link between the treasures of the past and the boats which are still active today, whether restored or recreated. What value should be attached to replicas, from the point of view of history and heritage, is not something I plan to discuss here. As will become apparent in these pages, preserving old racing boats is an activity which has extraordinary life. Recreations of lost racers have the merit of allowing us to relive forgotten sensations and techniques of piloting. Whether powered by an old engine, which gives them additional interest, or by a modern engine, they allow the practice of a living activity without the risk of irretrievable loss in the case of an accident.

As for actually piloting these boats and sharing the fun of it, one country shows the way to all the others. The most important collections are in the United States, and the reader should not be surprised by the number of American boats referred to in the text. The two last World Wars spared this country with its long-standing interest in the preservation of its technical heritage. Europe, on the other hand, is unfortunately represented mostly by archive pictures even though its technological and sporting contributions were fundamental throughout the period under consideration. Most of the racers from the Old Continent met their end by destruction, desecration or disuse. But fortunately, some important boats did survive, and the enthusiasm of a few people of vision has already saved a few of them; perhaps this book will inspire some more. At least things are already moving in the right direction.

I would also hope that this book may inspire researchers to dig more deeply into this immense subject, which deserves further exploration. Mistakes or imprecisions may well have crept into my text, constructed as it is from widely dispersed sources and evidence which is hard to find. My thanks go in advance to anyone who is able to correct what I have written.

Gérald Guétat

From One World to Another

THE INTERNAL COMBUSTION ENGINE WAS PERFECTED IN BOATS DURING THE 1880S. MARINE USE OF THIS NEW METHOD OF PROPULSION PRECEDED ITS USE ON LAND BY SEVERAL YEARS. FROM THE BEGINNING OF THIS CENTURY, SPEED-BOAT COMPETITIONS BECAME A WAY OF ATTRACTING CAR BUYERS.

Sagitta is a recreation of a displacement launch from the first decade of the century. She has a 320hp six-cylinder Fiat engine. Recreations of this kind allow us today to watch these mythical shapes in action and to see once again how they behaved. Elegant hulls like this one, which displaced tons of water, would soon give way to new types which planed across the surface of the water.

The hulls of the first fast pleasure boats were not innovatory, but were inspired by military or civilian examples. Real innovation lay in their engines. This book deals only with boats using internal combustion engines, and so does not cover steam propulsion.

A FEW FACTS AND FIGURES

It was the Frenchman Lenoir (in 1860) and the German Otto (in 1867) who perfected the internal combustion engine. Lenoir ran some trials on the Seine shortly before 1870, with a two-stroke engine with a low power output. There is no doubt that he can be credited with the first trials of this kind in a boat, but his engine was heavy and clumsy, and this limited the scope of his experiments. In 1872, the American Brayton conceived the idea of a petrol engine with constant compression, and it appears that he went on to try this out in a boat some time around 1880.

After the legal wrangles between Otto and Lenoir, the four-stroke cycle entered the public domain. Between 1882 and 1884, Lenoir abandoned his two-stroke engine and perfected a new one using the theories of Beau de Rochas, which he then fitted into a boat which reached a speed of 8.7mph in a demonstration run between Le Havre and Tancarville. At this point, the engineer Fernand Forest enters the story; he had designed a tramway engine but decided to try it out on water. So *Le Volapück*, whose iron hull had been used for experiments with electric motors, became the first motor boat and was tested in 1885 alongside the Quai de la Rapée in Paris. In 1886, the German pioneer Daimler tested one of his first four cycle engine in a lapstrake launch. A little later, Daimler's company began selling motor launches, one being built specially for the Kaiser. Soon after these engines would become famous when they appeared in racing cars.

Shortly after that, in 1888, Butler was conducting experiments in Germany,

and Lablin followed in 1889. Steam power continued to resist such attacks on its supremacy, but not for long. The internal combustion engine gradually demonstrated all its advantages, and the future of the modern power unit was founded on them. To some extent, the development of the car and of the aeroplane depended on boats, which provided engines for one and opened the way for seaplane variants of the other. So it was that at the beginning of the century, young naval engineers like Alphonse Tellier were building boats and seaplanes with floats whose shapes derived directly from research done on speed boats. For a number of years, it was work done on water which helped in the conquest of the air.

THE FIRST MOTOR BOAT REGATTAS

The first races of mechanically-propelled boats which involved a significant number of competitors seem to have been organized during the Universal Exhibition in 1867. But it was not until much later, at Harfleur in 1892, that this occasional nautical activity took on the trappings of a sport; then later at Nice, a race involving four boats fitted with four-cylinder Forest and Gallice engines caused some trouble.

What actually happened was that some local journalists announced a race on the occasion of a visit by some great yachts, and the public turned out in force to admire the majestic maneuvers of these magnificent sailing ships. But instead of the harmonious spectacle of a sailing regatta, the spectators were surprised to see a flotilla of little launches chasing one another nose to tail and backfiring noisily. Their first reaction was anger that they had been deceived, but the anger soon gave way to curiosity and this strange race finished amid public approval and enthusiasm. The habit of watching these small and smelly boats being put through their paces gradually became a custom, and the word "racer" was adopted into the everyday language.

The founding of the Hélice Club de France in 1896 was a decisive stage in the organization of this infant

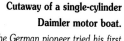

Cutaway of a single-cylinder Daimler motor boat.

The German pioneer tried his first engines out in launches, beginning in 1886. With their reversing devices removed, these same engines would later be fitted into cars.

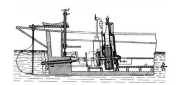

Three types of Forest engine. The one on the right, which has two cylinders and dates from 1886, is very similar to the one fitted into the pioneering motor boat, *Le Volapück*, in 1885.

The engine on the right also has two cylinders and magneto ignition, and dates from 1887. The engine in the center is a single-cylinder with cooling fins and dates from 1881.

Sectional view of the 1904 racer powered by a *Gardner-Serpollet* steam engine.

This company was the last to promote this type of engine in competition on water and on land, where Léon Serpollet won the Rothschild Cup in 1903 at the wheel of his steam-powered car.

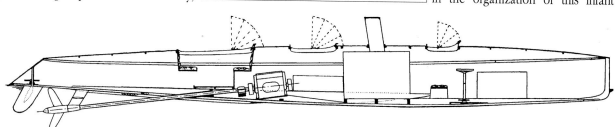

Fernand Forest's *Le Volapück* is generally considered to be the first motor boat. It was pictured near the Quai de la Rapée in 1885. The 6hp engine gave the boat a speed of 10mph and a fuel consumption of gallon per hour. Lenoir had in fact made some earlier demonstration runs between Le Havre and Tancarville between 1882 and 1884.

The experiments by Forest and other pioneers made Paris and the Seine into the world capital of motor boat activity at the turn of the century.

Marie is a replica of the first Daimler motor boat of 1886.

Successive developments of the engine in this boat became very successful in the first car races, particularly for Panhard et Levassor, who held the French license for Daimler engines.

The helmsman of this *Gardner-Serpollet* steam boat, No. 31, has donned a straw boater to protect himself from sun-stroke on the Seine.

The plume of white smoke in the background is from a passing steam tug giving a blast on its siren.

11

This picture shows preparations for the highly popular "Paris to the sea" race in 1908, in front of the de Coninck boatyard at Maisons-Lafitte.
The boat traveling from left to right across the picture is a prototype skimmer designed by the American Fauber.

The first racing boats had impressive-looking screws. These two were pictured in Monaco: left is the *Daimler II* (1907), and right the *Napier Siola* (1906).

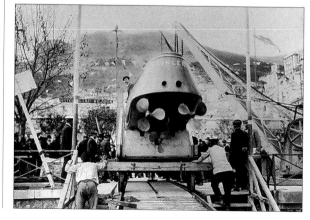

sport. On June 23 and 24, 1900, a race run under its aegis at Argenteuil showed the value of the regulations which had recently been drawn up. The stimulus had been provided, and the movement started to grow in France and in the neighboring countries until the real dawn of the twentieth century in 1914.

BIRTH OF THE GREAT CLASSICS

The great turning-point came in 1903. A number of major trials were organized in France, among them the first Dubonnet Cup and the 100km race at Poissy, where two boats distinguished themselves: the *Titan,* with a Delahaye engine, and the *Antoinette.* But there were some important initiatives from the English-speaking countries as well. This was the year when a group of enthusiastic Americans founded the American Power Boat Association, whose aim was to "promote speed trials to improve the construction of engines and the lines of boats . . ."

It was also in 1903 that Tiffany's in New York were commissioned to make the Gold Cup, which would become the prize in a speedboat competition the following year. At the same time, Alfred Harmsworth, proprietor of the British *Daily Mail,* put forward the British International Trophy. Better known as the Harmsworth Trophy, this was contested at the end of a major motor car competition, the Gordon Bennett Cup. This founding trophy was first contested on July 12, 1903 at Queenstown Harbour, near Cork in Ireland.

Speedboat racing attracted a lot of attention on both sides of the Atlantic, but there was an important difference of approach between the Europeans and the Americans. Europe was ahead of the United States in the development of cars, and the development of speedboat races was closely linked to the automobile industry, which was then making progress by leaps and bounds. In the United States, the new sport brought together the yachting tradition, technology and leisure, and appeared to be influenced less by the specialized interests of industrialists.

That may seem strange, because the Americans are regularly seen as being exclusively devoted to the expansion of industry and wealth. The first races of the famous American Gold Cup were organized on the Saint Lawrence, by a relatively small club, in a quiet summer resort region. On the Old Continent, it was clear that the Harmsworth Trophy and the completely new Monaco Meeting in 1904 were promotional events. In France, speedboat races soon followed the example of motor car racing, although there was great confusion over the multiplicity of technical regulations. At one meeting of the Automobile Club de France, a journalist made no bones about it: "Our clients are car builders and they want to put car engines into speedboats. So we must organize races for speedboats."

In 1904, road races were very expensive for motor car manufacturers, who turned to motor boats for their publicity, as F. Forest notes: *"And so the car makers were very*

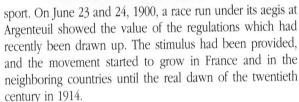

Georges Prade, on the left, organized the international Monaco Meeting from 1904.
This picture shows him in 1906 with Monsieur Cottonio, one of the owners of the twin-engined racer Caflit.

The Swiss motor boat *Martini III* was shown at the 1906 international Monaco Meeting. Her steel hull by Escher-Wyss was fitted with a 70bhp Martini petrol engine. Her bow spur is typical of fast naval boats at the end of the nineteenth century.
The shape of motor boat hulls was influenced for a long time by old-fashioned ideas. It was engines which mostly accounted for improvements in performance before the end of the first decade in the twentieth century.

13

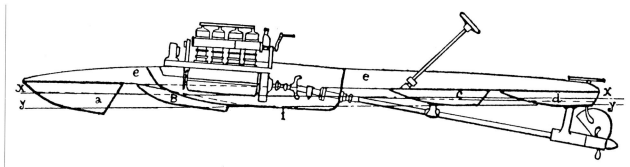

happy to discover a less financially demanding field of competition in boat racing. There were 100,000 Francs worth of prizes at the Monaco Meeting. An exhibition of boats preceded the ten days of racing which took place in beautiful countryside and attracted wealthy people. Nothing more was needed to get the car makers to come to Monaco."

Georges Prade was editor-in-chief of the magazine *Le Sport* and an adviser to Camille Blanc, president of the Société des bains de mer, and the two of them founded the international Meeting organized in the principality from 1904. Prade observed, *"For the first time, the whole world was interested in a motor boat race, and for the first time, a proper program allowed people to study all the possible marine applications of a light engine . . . For the first time, a 10-meter motor boat exceeded 20 knots in an hour, a speed which only a few large ships can reach. And by a coincidence which was really no more than a logical result, the engine which won the Cup presented by His Highness Prince Albert the First of Monaco turned out to be the one which had won the glorious Gordon Bennett Cup in France in a car three months later. This symbolized perfectly the direct application of a car engine in a motor boat."*

DOWN TO THE WATERFRONT

The Monaco Meeting was nevertheless not an isolated event, and the "Paris to the sea" race also became very popular when it was held for the second time in 1904. The crowd which invaded the steep banks of the Seine between the Neuilly and the Bineau bridges was estimated at more than 10,000 people. One important innovation introduced greater precision: a huge clock face with manually altered hands was set up on the pontoon at the starting line to show the official time. The great names which would become familiar in competition in Europe were there: Mercedes (whose engine was in a Pitre hull), Grégoire and Hotchkiss, as well as a lone

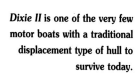

It takes skill and courage to pilot a motor boat with a displacement hull.

The American motor boat Turk *is seen here at full speed. This type of hull drenches its crew as soon as it begins to create waves, and can also roll from side to side in a most disconcerting fashion. The pilot is holding himself perfectly upright here, despite the angle the boat is taking in the turn.*

The entrepreneur Marius Dubonnet financed the construction of a racer powered by the Delahaye "Titan" engine, in preparation for the 1905 racing season. The Delahaye factory used the occasion to prepare a massive four-cylinder engine of 5190ci capacity which developed 350bhp, a considerable output for the time.

This engine was the first in the world to have twin overhead camshafts operating six valves per cylinder. Although her design did not allow her to make the best of this major technical advance, Le Dubonnet did break the world speed record for 1905, reaching 33.80mph on the lake at Juvisy, near Paris.

steam-powered entry from Gardner-Serpollet. This company had obtained some remarkable results with steam-powered cars, and on April 7 1903, Léon Serpollet won the Henri de Rothschild Cup for the third time, with a speed 7mph faster than any of his competitors while he was using no more than two-thirds of the power available.

In both Paris and Monaco, all the manufacturers threw themselves enthusiastically into the power race, including Napier from Britain, Fiat from Turin, and the French firms of Antoinette, Berliet, Grégoire, Brasier and Delahaye. The latter made the news with its huge steel-hulled motor boat powered by a 350bhp D. O. H. C. four-cylinder engine of 5190ci capacity—the same engine which had initially been in the motor boat *Le Dubonnet*. Competitive events began to spring up all over Europe, on Lake Garda, Lake Maggiore,

the Lac des Quatre-Cantons at Lucerne, and at Evian. Categories started to become well-defined, with the "unlimited" monsters designed purely for speed being separated from cruisers of different types designed to have real seagoing qualities in long-distance races. Owners were not afraid of taking these new vessels out on the high seas, and the first official offshore event seems to have been the Calais-Dover Race of 1904, followed by a madcap event between Algiers and Toulon in 1905 which turned into a drama. Generally, however, speedboats at the beginning of the century were not suited to deep sea navigation. Moreover, it could be argued that the great influence of the car makers' lobby over the early days of the speedboat actually held back advances in marine engines designed specifically for seagoing craft.

RACERS AND TORPEDO-BOATS

The first competitions made it clear that the internal combustion engine would overturn all the rules about hull design. In the words of the American designer Clinton Crane, the man behind the *Dixie* boats: *"The development of the internal combustion engine, which is very light for its power output, has permitted great progress in terms of speed on the water."* While torpedo boats—the fastest vessels of the day—seemed to have shown definitively that a long hull was a basic factor in achieving high speeds, racing boats

equipped with internal combustion engines achieved the same speeds with hulls a quarter the length. The French designer and builder Alphonse Tellier agreed entirely with this, and made some interesting comparisons: *"Scaling up the speed of the* Rapée III *would give an incredible 28mph for a ship the size of the* Deutschland. *[The* Rapée III*] has 80bhp per tonne of displacement, while Mr. Parsons' famous* Turbinia *has only 21.2hp per tonne even though it has the very lightest of steam engines."*

AN EXAMPLE: THE IRRESISTIBLE *DIXIE*

Dixie II was designed by Clinton Crane, whose talents embraced sailing yachts as well as motor boats. This new boat was designed specifically to defend the Harmsworth Trophy, which the first *Dixie* had won in 1907. *Dixie II* was built in 1908 at City Island by the highly regarded Wood boatyard. Her hull was tested in a hull tank, and her engine was designed by Clinton Crane's brother Henry, who was a car manufacturer. This was a 45-degree V8 unit which developed 220bhp at 900rpm and was designed specially for the boat. During her first trials on July 27, 1908, *Dixie II* achieved a speed of 35mph, and on August 3 easily won the Harmsworth Trophy with an average speed of 32mph. Her British adversary, the *Wolseley Siddeley*, had two engines of 200bhp each, while the *Daimler II* boasted three engines with a total of 525bhp. At the end of that same August, *Dixie II* outclassed six competitors to win the Gold Cup on the Saint Lawrence river, where her average speed was calculated at 30mph over three heats of thirty miles each. *Dixie II* also won the next two Gold Cup events, in 1909 and 1910.

CULTURE SHOCK AT MONACO

The news of the Monaco event crossed the Atlantic, and at the end of 1908 *Dixie II*'s owner asked his designer to sketch a new boat to compete there. Clinton Crane drew up a model which tests in the hull tank suggested would be 3 km/h faster than the earlier boat. The new boat was built by the boatyard of Geo Lawley and Sons in Boston and—strangely—carried the old name of *Dixie II*. Her splendid hull differed from the earlier boat's in a number of details, such as a shorter cockpit, a different ventilation system and a longer stern. So it seems that the boat which went to Monaco in 1909 was the new *Dixie*, which could be named Dixie III. But the American champion turned in a poor performance in this great European classic, taking an hour and 38 minutes to cover the 32 miles course while the winner, the *Wolseley Siddeley II*, finished in 49 minutes.

Dixie **took part in the 1909 Monaco event, the first and only time this exceptional line of American boats encountered setbacks.**

Conditions in the Mediterranean were very different from those on the rivers and lakes on the other side of the Atlantic.

The American boat was not suited to racing conditions in the Mediterranean. Its European rivals were 10 feet longer and boasted two or three times as much power. However, this was the only defeat ever suffered by the *Dixie* boats in their entire career. After the disappointment of Monaco, *Dixie II* returned to the charge and successfully defended the Harmsworth Trophy in 1910, which proved to be the last victory by a displacement boat in an event held in the English-speaking countries. The unsuccessful British challenger, *Pioneer,* was a Fauber type hydroplane with a top speed 9mph greater than *Dixie*'s.

THE END OF THE DINOSAURS

In 1909, a 290 feet torpedo boat was capable of 40mph. That year, the 40 feet-long *Dixie II* won the Gold Cup at 33mph. But the end for racing boats with displacement hulls came a year later. Despite the *Pioneer*'s failure to beat *Dixie,* the general impression was that the era of the displacement hull was coming to an end. As the designer George Crouch put it: *"1909 marks the end of experiments with displacement hulls for racing boats. Dixie II can be considered the most beautiful example of this type of boat design in America. At low speeds, these hulls are more efficient than hydroplanes with stepped hulls and concave vee shapes without a step. One of the great faults of displacement hulls like that of Dixie II is that the loss of stability at speed limits their ability to increase that speed and skim across the water. So these hulls demand incredible skill from their pilots if they are to reach their maximum speed."*

THE FIRST HYDROPLANES

It is difficult to date precisely the first researches into increasing the speed of boats by keeping them on the surface of the water. The most important work is generally attributed to the English priest, C. M. Ramus. In 1872, he proposed a new type of fast ship to the Admiralty: *"The object of this invention is to lift the ship out of the water by means of the resistance of the liquid at high speeds,"* and this was to be achieved by inclined planes. In Britain, the name of Thornycroft is linked to similar work from 1877, and then the name of Saunders shortly afterwards. On the continent, the Swiss Pictet published a thesis in 1883 on the subject of the

17

Suwanee **is an American launch of 1909. She has a displacement hull and is 31 feet long. The pilot's position shows the extreme simplicity of the controls.** *This boat has been preserved, but without her original engine.*

Archives of the physical and natural sciences in Geneva. But none of these theories could work without a complete reversal of the relationship between weight and power, as Clinton Crane noted: *"The very recent development of the petrol engine, which is very light in proportion to its power, has signaled the start of a new era in the conquest of high speeds on water. As far as speed is concerned, I think that the Reverend Ramus was simply born too soon."*

The French who had already made a fundamental contribution to engine development, were not sitting idly by. In 1891, the Comte de Lambert took out a patent for a planing hull which could be tried experimentally as soon as the beginning of the twentieth century brought motors powerful enough. One of his most effective models was 21.5 feet long and 10 feet wide, and consisted of a series of five inclined planes made of wood and aluminum. The engine was a 12hp twin-cylinder made by De Dion-Bouton, the total weight of the vessel was 800 pounds with one man on board, and a twin-blade variable-pitch propeller gave propulsion up to speeds of 7-10mph. The Count achieved officially verified speeds of 18 and later 25mph. To reach such speeds, boats of classic design needed 50bhp.

It All Started on the Seine

Fauber was an American citizen who decided to settle in Paris to take advantage of better working conditions. A Fauber hydroplane began to take shape in front of the de Coninck boatyard at Maisons-Lafitte in 1908, and in 1909 Fauber took out a very complex and practically incomprehensible patent which covered numerous aspects of hydroplane theory. His principal contribution was a combination of stepped hull with V-section, as the architect George Crouch described it: *"A boat with a displacement hull moves through the water; a hydroplane generally displaces considerably less than its own weight. The work done by Fauber in France after 1908 is extremely important, because it breaks with what had been done before. Its great contribution was to propose boats which are both fast and able to sail in a reasonable swell. If you fill the space between the steps of a Fauber hull, the result is a very good boat and practically a concave V with a very modern appearance."*

The impression left by the first hydroplanes on the pilots of boats with displacement hulls is astonishing: *"left standing as if we were at anchor"* was a typical comment. Instead of forcing its way through the liquid mass, the hydroplane skims across its surface, and its essential characteristic is to displace less than its own weight of water.

It is instructive to compare some speeds: at Monaco in 1904, the winner was the displacement boat *Trèfle à quatre*, at 25.9mph; in 1908, again at Monaco, the *Panhard Levassor* classical type reached 33.1mph; in summer 1912, the American hydroplane *Reliance III* with only 150bhp reached

53.7mph over the official distance of one mile. The international career of hydroplanes really began in 1911 at the Harmsworth Trophy event with the British boat *Pioneer*, which beat the *Dixie IV*. Right up until the 1914 war, displacement boats continued to battle against very big hydroplanes descended directly from the earlier types, and against a new generation of very small boats.

The last time the Harmsworth Trophy was held before the war was in 1913. That year, *Baby Reliance III* represented the archetypical hydroplane with a single step. Her direct rival, the monster British boat *Maple Leaf IV* owned by Sir Tommy Sopwith, showed the evolution of the traditional boat towards the hydroplane. She was 40 feet long and had two 12-cylinder engines of 740bhp. Against this, the little American boat *Baby Reliance III* was just 20 feet long with a 150bhp Sterling engine; she was faster but more fragile, and broke down in the rough British waters.

In 1914, *Baby Speed Demon* beat the Gold Cup record in the United States with a speed of 51.72mph, but engines were still heavy and not very powerful, with low crankshaft speeds and extremely low compression ratios. So the hydroplane was catching on decisively on the eve of the First World War, but it still needed a new generation of engines which were both light and powerful.

Farewell to boats with displacement hulls. The attractive lines and elegant deportment of these splendid launches could not compensate for their lack of speed in comparison with hydroplanes from the beginning of the century's second decade.

A few rare and original examples like Rosalind still exist to bear witness to an era which drew to a close with the First World War.

The Wings of Victory

THE LONG, SLEEK RACING SPEEDBOATS OF THE TURN OF THE CENTURY DISAPPEARED AS WAR DESTROYED THE OLD EUROPEAN ORDER. THE BRILLIANT CIVILIZATION OF THE PAST WAS THREATENED WITH EXTINCTION. HAD THE CREATIVE DARING AND INGENUITY OF THE MECHANICAL PIONEERS DONE NO MORE THAN PREPARE FOR THE FIGHTING?

Miss Minneapolis, seen (left) at over 60mph, was the archetypal stepped-hull hydroplane. Note the cheek of the rudder, which is positioned well forwards. By 1916, the days of racing boats with marine engines were numbered. The Liberty engine, seen below in a De Havilland DH4, was soon to conquer all its rivals.

In 1916, *Miss Minneapolis* was the first racer officially to break the mile a minute barrier. This was achieved on a course one terrestrial mile long, over which the boat traveled six times without stopping.

This hydroplane won the Gold Cup that same year. It was powered by a 250hp Sterling eight cylinder in-line marine engine with overhead valves. At this period worldwide standards for speed events were still a long way off, which is why it is often difficult to credit a given competitor with an absolute record.

Miss Minneapolis makes her way slowly towards a speed run. The pilot and the mechanic seem tense as they prepare to withstand the enormous power of the rumbling machinery in front of them.

At low speeds, a hydroplane sits low in the water. At speed, the hull gradually rises until it is skimming across the water, thus greatly reducing the drag of the liquid.

The conquest of speed on the water had become a civilian pursuit. Small racing boats had managed to equal and then exceed the performance of the torpedo boats and fast patrol boats. From the beginning of the century's second decade, the winners of the major contests had boats which skimmed along the surface of the water; and right up until the beginning of World War 1 both sides of the Atlantic saw competition between large hydroplanes over 33 feet long and small boats which were only just longer than they were wide, and where almost the only thing visible was the black mass of the engine. In America the best of these hulls were the disarmingly simple creations of a small craftsman called Chris Smith. His Christian name—which would later become associated with the word "craft"—dominated the motor boat scene after 1914. Often named *Baby* this or *Miss* that, his boats were unbeatable on the water in the New World.

In 1915, a group of Detroit residents, enthusiastic supporters of their city, decided to finance the construction of a racing boat. Among them were a number of automobile makers. The aim of the Miss Detroit Powerboat Association was to officially break the 60mph barrier and to win the famous Gold Cup. These new businessmen from the Great Lakes area had great hopes of breaking the domination of the East Coast and of the arrogant New York metropolis.

Chris Smith was in some financial difficulty as the result of an excessive addiction to poker, and he was the inspiration behind this challenge from the Motor City, which of course ensured that he would build a new boat. *Miss Detroit I* was, like all his creations, a single-step hydroplane, apparently without any particular new features. It had a 250hp six-cylinder Sterling engine. Together with their rivals from van Blerck, these engines completely dominated competition at the time.

MACHINERY WITH THE POWER TO THRILL

The Gold Cup was organized at Manhasset Bay, near New York, and *Miss Detroit I* won easily against *Baby Speed Demon*

At rest, *Miss Minneapolis* shows that only a footrest separates the crew from the huge engine.

The throttles are opened by a simple shaft on the left of the steering wheel. The original version, built in 1916 for the season's racing, was not as well finished as this.

Faced with competition from *Miss Minneapolis* in 1916, *Miss Detroit* was unable to retain the Gold Cup she had won the previous year. Nevertheless there was not a lot of difference between the two boats, which was why *Miss Detroit* tried her luck again in 1917.

These were the products of Chris Smith's small boatyard, which constructed the fastest American racers. The rivalry between the cities on the East Coast and the Midwest gave him the chance to build a new boat each year, each one slightly better than the last. After 1914, his single-step hydroplanes reached an unequaled state of perfection; they skimmed perfectly flat across the surface of the water. In addition, improvements made on hulls at the time made little difference because engines were becoming more and more powerful, which was enough to increase performance from one year to the next.

II, which belonged to Mrs. Paula Blackston, the wife of a film industry pioneer. The trophy went west and only returned east ten years later. Detroit's success whetted the appetites of other industrial cities in the Mid-West. In 1916 Chris Smith built *Miss Minneapolis*, which can be seen as the archetype of the single-step hydroplane, as well as the archetype of all unlimited class boats in the next ten years.

Since 1911 Chris Smith had been perfecting the principle of the single-step hull. This step was a simple right angle which broke the line of the keel about half way between the stem and the stern. All the Smith hydroplanes had long front sections and flat planning areas where they skimmed across the water. The hull skimmed almost perfectly, flat for its whole length, so that no appreciable improvement in performance could be expected without increasing the power of the engine. The string of victories by the *Miss* boats intrigued the specialists, and when they were exhibited at

boat shows they were chastely veiled below the water line; so some visitors pretended to have dropped something and tried to look under the hull. One of the most highly regarded boat designer of racing boat history, George F Crouch, described these astonishing machines in these words: "*Most of the space in these relatively short boats is taken up by the engine, which leaves only a little room for the pilot and mechanic [. . .]. The huge engine has straight-through exhausts, and the exhaust pipe for each cylinder rises less than a foot high above the engine. To get the best out of such boats needs a pilot of above average skill, and as soon as the water becomes choppy the boat is very difficult to steer.*"

It was true that winning trophies and breaking speed records with engines which were becoming more and more powerful demanded a great deal of courage. On board a racer like *Miss Minneapolis* for example, the crew sat very low, less than 12 inches above the water with their backs against the stern, and with a fierce backwash right behind them. The throttle was a simple shaft, and there was no decking or protection of any sort behind the engine. Their feet rested on an unstable wooden slat made slippery by leaked oil. Both pilot and mechanic had to hang on tight in order to stay in the boat, and the man holding the wheel had a decisive advantage in this. The intrepid pair wore padding on their thighs and shins. If they were not to be thrown overboard by the acceleration, by the force of the waves hitting the boat or by centrifugal force in the turns, they had to wedge a leg under deck sides which doubled as an arm rest.

ON THE WAY TO MISSISSIPPI

Miss Minneapolis completely trounced *Miss Detroit* by three heats to one and took the Gold Cup. Shortly afterwards, at the national championship trials held over a one mile course, the new *Miss* made six runs at an average of 61.083mph. Establishing the exact time for speed records continued to pose problems until the beginning of the 1920s.

This was the case in the United States with the all-important 60mph barrier; the mile in question was a terrestrial mile of 1,609 meters. *Miss Minneapolis*, often credited with this record, was in fact the second boat to have broken the mythical barrier. In 1915, *Disturber IV*, a 40 feet Fauber type hydroplane built for the 1914 Harmsworth Trophy which was canceled because of the war, was officially timed at 60.75mph over a half-mile course. *Disturber IV* had two in-line 12 cylinder Duesenberg engines with a total power output of more than 1,500hp.

In these years boat owners and some journalists were quick to attribute records, most often unofficial ones. In the absence of strict regulations, especially concerning the distances covered to establish a time, we now have to be very careful when it comes to making comparisons. The spectators at motor boat races usually focused on the idea of a mile a minute, which is easy to compare with the speed of a car or a train. So it is arguable that, as far as the almost theological question of the 60mph barrier is concerned, *Disturber IV* broke it over the half-mile in 1915, while *Miss*

Speedboat racing was an enjoyable civilian pursuit, but speed on the water was also a military necessity. Hydroplanes owned by the authorities patrolled the Atlantic coast; this patrol boat was launched in January 1917 by the Loew Victor Company.

Speedboat racing was an important factor in the development of hulls which skimmed the surface of the water. For this reason, fast launches built at the time of the First World War show structural trends which are very similar to those of the racers.

The New World threw itself enthusiastically into the conflict. In a patriotic and generous gesture, a uniformed Uncle Sam holds out a helping hand to the besieged French officer. When circumstances required it, American artists willingly took part in the war effort, as witness this poster for a successful musical comedy of winter 1917.

The Atlantic Ocean is shown as a river. On it are the ships sent to help, while the aircraft above symbolize the wings of hope. America was ill-prepared for war, but its huge material and human resources swung the balance of power in Europe.

Minneapolis did so in 1916 over the mile. After 1917 of course, the sport moved on so quickly that there was no longer any need to split hairs in this way.

THE FINAL VICTORY BY A MARINE ENGINE

The victory of *Miss Minneapolis* in 1916 clearly marked the end of an era—she was the last boat equipped with a marine engine to win the Gold Cup—and it saw the beginning of a relationship between Chris Smith and a young pilot called Gar Wood. After their meeting, nothing would ever be the same again. Garfield Wood came from the Great Lakes region, which had been the cradle of mechanical industry's growth. He was very young, with a passionate interest in speed on the water and engines. Around 1911, he invented a hydraulic system for unloading lorries which made his fortune. He settled in Detroit, in the heart of the Motor City where the carmaking empires were born. Gar Wood was bold, skillful and headstrong. He had considerable wealth, and his personality made a deep imprint on every chapter of speedboat racing history between 1917 and 1933.

Things became serious for this young millionaire in 1915 after the victory of *Miss Detroit I*. Gar Wood bought the boat and was beaten by the Minneapolis team using the 1916 Chris Smith boat. He took *Miss Detroit I's* defeat by *Miss Minneapolis* hard, and decided to have *Miss Detroit II* built, joining forces with Chris Smith to guarantee the exclusive services of the best boatyard. In 1917, the Gold Cup was hurriedly organized on the Mississippi river, and *Miss Minneapolis*, defending the trophy, was fitted with an aero engine. This blew up on trial, and the faithful six-cylinder Sterling marine engine was reinstalled. But the outgoing winner no longer had the support of her inspired builder. Nothing could prevent the daring Gar Wood from winning the trophy, assisted by his engineer Jay, who was Chris Smith's brother.

The original *Arab IV* was a 1916 stepped-hull hydroplane which was successful until 1920, when she sank during a race. Her owner, a Mr. Sidway, was a horseracing man. *The new Arab IV has the same 21 feet length as the original, and her current 500hp Chevrolet V8 engine has similar power to the V12 aero engine which was fitted in the original boat at the end of her career.*

Pictured in August 1917, *Peter Pan VIII* is a good example of a racing hydroplane. The two tough-looking crew members appear ready for anything behind the 250hp in-line eight-cylinder Sterling engine, whose straight-through exhausts discharge just above their heads.

This boat was the work of the great George Crouch, one of the pioneers of planing hulls and of the so called three-point keels, who said of such craft: "Races were often canceled if there was a swell because the punishment inflicted on the crews in these conditions was too great." Marine engines like the one seen here were nearing the end of their racing days; aero engines were about to take over.

Nevertheless, *Miss Detroit II* did not appear very different from her predecessor. Each new Smith hydroplane brought only slight improvements over its predecessor; it always skimmed the water better and simply went a little faster. The achievements of the boats from Algonac in Michigan gradually and methodically improved after the beginning of the century's second decade, but the great strides made in engine design during the war and the phenomenal expansion of aviation after 1916 and 1917 completely transformed the relationship between power and shape.

AVIATION BRINGS WAR INTO THE TWENTIETH CENTURY

Military air power was born with the First World War. In August 1914, the warring sides had just 800 aircraft between them, and in 1918 more than 200,000 aircraft would be built to train pilots, make up squadrons and replace losses. France built most of these—more than 50,000 aircraft and

When the United States entered the war on April 6, 1917, a lot of young men inspired by speed and daring seized their chance to become involved with the romantic adventure of aviation.

In the second row of this picture taken on an aerodrome are Caleb Bragg (without a hat) and Jesse Vincent (wearing a leather flying helmet).

Caleb Bragg was famous as a racing driver in his native country before he became involved with aviation during the First World War and then with speedboat racing.

He commonly used European machinery imported to the United States. This picture shows him driving a Fiat on a dusty road, before he became involved in the purchase of a license for Hispano-Suiza aero engines for the Wright Company.

29

90,000 engines, many of them destined for her allies. Before the war the Hispano-Suiza Company built nothing but cars, but in Barcelona in autumn 1914 the marque's co-founder, Swiss engineer Marc Birkigt, designed an aero engine using the latest technology. By February 1915 a 150hp V8 engine with remarkably pure lines was running on the test-bed. Birkigt's major innovations were aluminum crankcases with detachable hardened steel cylinders and fully-lubricated direct-acting valves with thick rods. Development was not without its difficulties but in July 1915 the first 150hp engine successfully passed its 10-hour certification at the Chalais-Meudon test center. Production got under way slowly, and the engine did not reach the front line until a year later, in August 1916. By increasing the crankshaft speed and the compression ratio, the initial model's power was increased to 180hp. It was this type 180 CV which powered most French fighter planes, notably the famous SPAD which excited the crowds when flown by the likes of Guynemer and Rickenbacker.

In 1917 the Americans flung their whole industrial and demographic might into the conflict and tipped the balance towards victory. They had almost no fighters, and as a result young Americans flew French aircraft at the front. It is noteworthy that many champion racing drivers were involved in various ways in the war in the air. The name of Rickenbacker was already written on the facade of the Miller factory in California, which made the carburetors fitted to the Peugeot cars raced by the popular drivers Resta and Rickenbacker, who completely dominated Indianapolis and the other speedways before the war.

Some of these pilots went on to play a lasting role in the development of speedboat racing when peace returned. Among them was Caleb Bragg, the winner of several events at the wheel of his Fiat. He was deeply involved with the industrial combine which took on the Hispano-Suiza manufacturing license to compensate for the weakness of the US aeronautics industry. The license granted to the Wright Company by the European firm contributed to the lasting success of the

The First World War gave aviation an extraordinary boost. The first 150hp Hispano-Suiza V8 engine developed in Spain by Marc Birkigt was homologated by the French authorities in July 1915. This engine was very advanced for its time and was taken up to 180hp for fighter aircraft, among them the famous SPAD of the Stork squadron.

Successive versions saw power increase to 200 and then 220hp. Some 50,000 engines of this type were built in France and abroad as the result of a vast program of manufacture under license.

THE WINGS OF VICTORY

In 1917 American war planes had no engine powerful and flexible enough to meet the needs of the European conflict. According to legend, engineers Vincent and Hall drew up the range of Liberty engines over a few days in a Washington hotel room. The most notable of these was the V12.** *The Liberty V12 had a capacity of 650ci and developed 420hp at 1,750rpm. At the end of the war the American government had some 12,000 surplus engines; when these were taken up by speedboat racers, they set off a revolution in racing for which the U.S. government was indirectly responsible.*

The first of the Liberty engines was this 350hp V8 built by Buick in 1917. *It was fitted into the hydroplane Liberty the Second, which sank during a race and remained under water for 62 years before being raised and restored.*

Hispano V8, of which 50,000 examples in all would be made by more than 20 factories in France and abroad.

SIX DAYS FOR VICTORY

The American war effort was considerable, particularly in aviation, an area which had been much neglected. The America of the Wright brothers had built only 600 aircraft, and barely a third of these had been military training aircraft; none were suitable for bombing or as fighter or observation aircraft. It made a distressing contrast with the Old Continent, where the aeronautics industry, especially in France, had been developing in a spectacular fashion since the beginning of the century. American aero engines were heavy, not very powerful and built in very small numbers; and so it was imperative to make a modern engine with multiple uses as quickly as possible. Two engineers came forward to develop this new engine: they were Jesse G Vincent, the chief engineer of Packard, and Elbert John Hall, of the Hall Scott Motor Car Company. The two men already had

This picture was taken in the *parc fermé* during the 1918 Gold Cup. In the foreground is *Miss Detroit III* with her first aero engine, a Curtiss V12. A cameraman is filming Gar Wood's team, which would dominate the race.

At the top of the picture, on the left, spectators are sitting alongside the Detroit river where the events were held. The large number of natural inland waterways in certain parts of America proved very favorable for the development of speedboats.

some schemes which they would have loved to sell to the government, but their projects did not correspond to the specifications put forward by the authorities.

The Americans did not have the experience of aerial combat which would have allowed them to define the characteristics of the future engine; and so a French delegation was invited to Washington in April 1917. Its advice was to reduce the durability and safety factors in favor of speed and power. With these recommendations in mind, Vincent and Hall set themselves up in a suite of rooms at a big Washington hotel and stayed there for six days. This luxurious improvised design office witnessed the birth of a light and powerful engine, a 225hp liquid-cooled V8. On the basis of this modular V8 with its components standardized

for mass production, it was possible to build engines with four, six, eight or twelve cylinders. Thus was the Liberty engine range born.

The prototype of the V8, which was the most immediately important, was built in four weeks. Under the masterly direction of the Packard factories, a whole network of builders and sub-contractors in the car industry was drafted in to help in this operation. Dodge, Cadillac, Hudson and Pierce Arrow all worked non-stop. The 225hp V8 had barely reached the test-bed before the army (the airforce was then a division of the army) demanded a V12 with a minimum of 400hp. And so the famous Liberty V12 came into being. In a few months, Packard, Lincoln, Cadillac, Ford, Marmon and Buick built more than 20,000

engines whose career lasted well beyond the 1914-18 war. Liberty engines were found in civil aircraft, in racing boats and in the great runabouts, and even in record-breaking cars like the famous *Babs* of the Welsh racing driver Parry Thomas. The Liberty engine remained associated with American military projects right up to 1945, the date when the Sparkman and Stephens partnership designed a rescue boat for naval pilots, powered by two marinized 500hp V12 Liberty engines. After 1918, the story of speedboat competition was also profoundly changed by the existence of a huge surplus of these engines, which were light, powerful and cheap.

GAR WOOD INITIATES THE ARMS RACE

George F Crouch described in these words the twin effects on competition of Gar Wood and the war: *"The major turning point came in 1918, when a new era began. Gar Wood, who won in 1917, retained the cup in 1918 with* Miss Detroit III. *What was new was not particularly the hulls or the means*

of propulsion or steering. Rather was it the use of aero engines, which were very powerful and very light. In 1918 you could see the first signs of an evolution which would completely change the world of speedboat racing in the ten years which followed."

There was in fact no restriction on boats permitted to take part in the great events. All those which had used heavy and relatively underpowered marine engines were fitted with aero engines, particularly Liberty V12s. Gar Wood bought a large number of these engines, which had been rapidly marinized, and in doing so fired the starting pistol for a race towards military sources and towards power. George F Crouch continued his analysis of the end of the century's second decade and of its excesses in the following words: *"These boats were unequaled for racing, but after one season's competition they were worthless. Moreover, conditions on board were so harsh that races often had to be canceled and there were many mechanical failures. The number of participants could get reduced to almost none, and the* length of the races could increase with the changes in the weather [. . .]. With the powerful Liberty engines sold as surplus by the American Government at less than one third of their value, people obtained outputs of over 500bhp and screw speeds of nearly 3,000rpm. Until these engines became available, marine engines dominated the scene. The arrival of the Liberty was overwhelming but it did not benefit everybody. Restrictions soon had to be imposed if the development of speedboats was not to be stifled altogether. It would be interesting to establish a class for boats which could be used for something other than pure racing."

The ones who did benefit from the Liberty engine were not too concerned about any eventual future restrictions; they tried to put together the largest possible number of very powerful engines into simple hulls which became faster and faster. While the Old Continent was just beginning to recov-

er from the terrible human and material destruction of the war, Gar Wood threw down the gauntlet to the British in 1919: he wanted to win back the most coveted motor boat trophy in the world, the British International Trophy. This work of art had been miraculously saved when the yacht carrying it caught fire and sank. To win the trophy Wood had the first *Miss America* built.

Gar Wood made no bones about his technical and sporting ambitions. He wanted to be the world's fastest man on water. His decision to go and race in Britain after 1920 was an important one. It made him, on the level of boat racing, an exact reflection of the new status which the United States had acquired at the end of the war. America had become the leading world power. The trophy was a symbol of Britain's past power, and the name of the new boat intended to take it away from Britain was symbolic of the

The great motor boat races attracted tens of thousands of spectators. The exploits of their heroic pilots fascinated the crowds, especially in the great industrial regions which were the home of the car industry's expansion.

The crowd is taking a close interest in the performance of the competing boats. Telegraph boards carried very detailed results, which were useful for the placing of discrete but lucrative bets

new spirit which motivated those on the other side of the Atlantic. Bearing as it did the name of *Miss America*, it could not be allowed to be beaten, and there could be no mistakes in its preparation. In this respect the team put together by the Wood brothers and the Smith brothers was exemplary. The new boat was shown in the course of construction during the winter of 1919 fitted with a single Liberty V12 engine. Gar Wood was cunning and the equally sharp Chris Smith willingly demonstrated modesty and discretion, so no-one could exclude the possibility that this was a tactic intended to confuse British observers about the final characteristics of the American challenger.

Whip-po-Will, Jr. is seen here being unloaded before the **1918 Gold Cup in Detroit. Note the step in the hull, positioned just ahead of where the propeller shaft emerges, and the rudder, under the front third of the boat.**
This hydroplane was designed with plenty of volume and was 28 feet long. She had two six-cylinder marine engines made by Van Blerck—the great rival of the unbeatable Sterling—with a total output of 565hp.

35

Miss America, the first boat to bear this name, was built for Gar Wood over the winter of 1919. Her owner had then just issued a challenge to the British, who since 1913 had held the coveted British International Trophy, also known as the Harmsworth Trophy.

Her builder, Chris Smith, concealed the very simple keel of this boat behind a cloth, as he always did at exhibitions. The boat had two Liberty V12 aero engines, but was pictured here in unfinished condition at the National Motor Boat Show in February 1920.

The Peace Dividends

AN UNPRECEDENTED ERA OF PROSPERITY OPENED FOR THE UNITED STATES WHILE EUROPE FLOUNDERED IN ENDLESS SOCIAL TROUBLES AFTER THE WAR. THE POWER RACE DOMINATED ALL THE WORLD'S GREAT SPEEDBOAT TROPHIES. CIRCUMSTANCES DIFFERED GREATLY FROM ONE SIDE OF THE ATLANTIC TO THE OTHER, BUT PEOPLE ON BOTH SIDES BEGAN TO WONDER IF THERE WAS A POINT TO ALL THIS.

Miss America was a symbol of the offensive announced in 1920 by Gar Wood, aimed at the total domination of competition with his Unlimited class boats. Two years later Smith and Vincent inaugurated a new and wiser era of the Gold Cup.

In spring 1919, the Americans took to the streets to celebrate their victory in the First World War. In New York, tons of ticker-tape and torn up telegrams were scattered over the parades on Fifth Avenue. President Thomas Woodrow Wilson preached dreams of greatness to the young League of Nations which would form part of a new world order, full of promise and stimulated by the United States.

But while Old Europe counted its dead and tried to sweep away its piles of ruins, the American nation quickly became tired of the world's problems. The war had fundamentally changed the moral outlook of a whole generation of young people, who now set out in search of new freedoms. In America, celebrations and economic development were the order of the day. Sport, particularly sport involving engine power, set free an enormous energy generated by the tensions of the world-wide conflict. Motor boat racing expressed the new spirit of conquest, in the lust for power sparked by the arrival on the market of large numbers of cheap surplus aero engines which were both light and powerful. At the end of 1919, speedboat champion Gar Wood challenged the British for the oldest and most coveted trophy, the British International Trophy, commonly known as the Harmsworth Trophy after its donor. The race was set up for the summer of 1920. From now on, the weakness of Old Europe would become evident.

In January 1920, the British Motor Boat Club announced a new category for 30-foot boats, which joined the existing one for 21-foot boats. The cylinder capacity of these boats had to be between 151 and 83ci. The idea was to inject new life into the moribund speedboat racing scene by establishing rules which were not too restrictive and favored the use of relatively cheap car engines. The magazine *Le Yacht* recorded its views enthusiastically on January 24 1920:

Activity on the deck of the *SS Adriatic* before she left New York for Britain on 2 July 2, 1920. The three American challengers for the Harmsworth Trophy can be seen stowed on the foredeck. Miss America's two V12 engines remain uncovered and can be seen in the left foreground. On the right of the picture is the rounded form of Whip-Po-Will, Jr, and alongside that the long silhouette of Miss Detroit V.

Who says that Gar Wood was only interested in the brute power of a Liberty V12? *This picture shows him crewing an elegant sailing boat with Charles Chapman, who is at the helm.*

"There is nothing new about the 183ci engine. Motor racing has already used it successfully and this relatively small capacity has allowed people to obtain very high power outputs which gave rise to remarkable speeds at the last Indianapolis meeting."

However in that same issue, *Le Yacht* also bore witness to the enormous economic and political difficulties then facing Europe, and France in particular, after the war. The next Monaco event was scheduled for April, but the International Sporting Club changed the rules so that the competitors did not have to equip their boats with reverse gear for the 1920 event. The Club invoked *"the exceptional circumstances in which industry finds itself, the coal crisis and the raw material crisis making it impossible to enforce the rule in full."*

September 1920, in Detroit. The judges are about to announce the results of the Gold Cup, which has been won by Gar Wood, seen standing and wearing a life jacket. The officials' work is being watched by his mechanic, Jay Smith, brother of the man who built the winning boat.

At the microphone is Charles Chapman of the American Power Boat Association. On the right, the two men in the boat are carrying a loud speaker.

41

From the start of the 1920s, interest in motor boats took off in the United States. The same formula applied in all sectors of the economy: everything had to be available, everywhere and at all times. This floating workshop owned by Fred Knight was pictured in 1921 and was offering "People's Gasoline," day and night.

America's abundant inland waterways allowed the country to develop a very active waterside lifestyle. In this picture, the banks are covered by houses and boathouses. Right in the middle of the river, a canoe has been hoisted out of the water for some attention on board this floating service station.

So these years saw a minimum level of activity in continental Europe. The Monaco meeting which opened the season heralded the return of the great competitions of the pre-war period, and was the only one that seemed likely to gather an interesting entry, even if it was a rather diverse one. There were events for four categories, and for some competitors these were preceded by a cruiser race from Lyons to Avignon, Toulon and Monaco. This was open to cruisers, the new 21 foot class of the British Motor Boat Club, Unlimited class racers and skimmers driven by aircraft propellers. The event was also open to seaplanes. The new major Monaco meeting of April 1920 was postponed by a week because of industrial unrest in certain factories which affected the suppliers of some competitors; in addition, there was a rail strike and a miners' strike in the coal producing regions.

France's Third Republic celebrated its fiftieth anniversary in a troubled social atmosphere. Germany had been crushed by the Treaty of Versailles and was suffering revolutionary convulsions. On April 2, 1920, French soldiers marched into the Ruhr—and the competition on the Riviera was not enough to make people forget the depressing situation around them. The event finished with the easy victory of racers from the Despujols boatyard,

powered by British Sunbeam engines, which took three of the first four places; third place went to the *Nieuport* with a Hispano engine.

THE AMERICANS HAVE LANDED

The great confrontation between the two worlds took place during the summer of 1920. The British had held the Harmsworth Trophy since before the war and were bent on preventing the Americans from getting their hands on it. Also present on the Solent were French and Spanish competitors. Between July 24, and August 4 the British selected their defenders. Sir Edgar Mackay's *Maple Leaf V*, a 40 feet boat with four 450hp Sunbeam engines, beat both Louis Coatalen's *Sunbeam Despujols,* a Franco-British boat which symbolized the *entente cordiale,* and a second *Maple Leaf,* number *VI.* The other competitors withdrew.

On the American side, three boats were loaded onto the steamship *Adriatic* in New York on July 2, 1920, on their way to Britain. Garfield Wood's *Miss Detroit V,* G. Wood Jr., his four-year-old son's boat *Miss America I,* and Mr. Judson's older racer *Whip-Po-Will* traveled together. The individual characteristics of the three challengers, as compared to those of the defender, show that the first American challenge was not all down to brute force. Quite the contrary, in fact.

All the competitors were hydroplanes with single-step hulls. The British *Maple Leaf V* was a twin-screw Saunders boat with 1800hp. Gar Wood, whose surplus V12 Liberty engines had ensured his supremacy across the Atlantic, prepared his attempt carefully by ordering two new boats from Chris Smith. Even though he equipped them for the first time with two Liberty engines giving a total of 800hp, their power seemed quite modest when compared to that of the British team. In fact, the American strategy was essentially based on sailing conditions, because the race would take place at sea and not on a river as in the United States. *Miss Detroit V* was an 38 feet boat, while *Miss America I* was only 26 feet long. To win the Harmsworth Trophy in average weather conditions, the ideal boat would fall mid-way between these two sizes. But Gar Wood had a large supply of Liberty engines, and he decided not to settle for a middle course; his plan was to have a large boat for rough conditions and a smaller one for calm conditions.

The third challenger shipped on board the *Adriatic* had two Bugatti-Duesenberg 16-cylinder engines (two eight-cylinder in-line engines joined together), each of 450bhp. This sophisticated motive power was produced under a manufacturing license for Bugatti aero engines which the

The era of full mechanization had begun. The engine was the new king of Republican America and had to be honored by its faithful servants everywhere.

This tanker lorry belonging to the Texaco company was pictured delivering its precious cargo in 1921.

Carl Fisher, one of the owners of the Indianapolis raceway, proposed a motor boat trophy reserved for boats which could be used outside competition. He was pictured here in the 1921 Fisher-Allison Trophy, piloting his boat *Aye Aye Sir*, magnificently built by the well-known Purdy boatyard.

It became necessary to place restrictions on competition for several reasons. Among them was the fragility of the open-hulled monsters with their huge, naked aero engines which dominated racing after the example of Gar Wood.

Meteor V was a competitor in the 1922 Gold Cup, which was run under new rules. It still has its original 26 feet hull, which carries a 300bhp Hispano-Suiza-Wright V8 engine.

John Hacker's design illustrates the new shape of racing boats designed to meet the new regulations. On the right, the open exhausts of the wild Arab IV, a Gold Cup entrant of an older generation, cast a shadow on the hull of this gentleman's racer.

United States had taken out during the war. Unfortunately, during the initial trials off the Isle of Wight, a petrol pipe burst and the boat caught fire immediately and sank. The crew were saved without serious injury.

The final tests for the trophy quickly went Gar Wood's way. Damage to the British boats and favorable sea conditions gave a total victory to *Miss America I* and the Wood team. The Harmsworth Trophy had been in British hands for nine years after being won in 1913 by Tommy Sopwith's *Maple Leaf IV*. Now it left Britain, never to return as a trophy of this unique speed test. Back in the United States again, *Miss America I* won the other great trophy of the early days, the Gold Cup, with an extraordinary average speed of 69.6mph.

FAVORABLE HYDROGRAPHY IN THE UNITED STATES

After the victory, America evolved swiftly in this new era of economic prosperity. Petrol was king, and with it the engine in all its applications; service stations multiplied; the modern car gave great freedom thanks to its ever-increasing reliability, and the arrival of solid roofs and opening side windows ensured that even bad weather was no longer a reason not to travel.

The use of motor boats also took off in an unprecedented fashion. The North American continent had a major geophysical advantage in this area: an abundant supply of inland waterways and lakes in almost all the states of the Union. Great rivers and immense lakes linked to one another by broad navigable waterways made this country a paradise for devotees of pleasure boating. Complete cities rose up around

the lakes, and even modest houses had a small wooden boathouse directly on the water. The motor boat quickly became the natural compliment to the car, providing its owners with a means of enjoyment as well as a means of commuting. Water thus afforded the freedom which the road often no longer provided, and the vast stretches of inland water set the speedboat on an almost endless course of development.

A MEETING MISSED IN DETROIT

The situation was strikingly different on the other side of the Atlantic. Against a background of miners' strikes and endemic social problems, the Monaco event of April 1921 remained the leading race meeting on the continent. Even so, its scope was modest; there were very few competitors and not many interesting innovations. Sea conditions were hard; there were just five entries in the unrestricted class and of these only three achieved a classification. The winner was the *Nieuport I*, followed by the *Cantieri Baglietto*. The magazine *Le Yacht* described the race in its inimitable inflated style and attributed its modest results to the crisis *"of the car industry, which we hope will be transitory."* The magazine also deplored the absence of British competitors at the event, but the British, upset by the loss of their Harmsworth Trophy, were preparing to cross the Atlantic and take their revenge. A new *Maple Leaf*, this time number *VII*, was built at the Saunders boatyard. She was just 3 feet shorter than its predecessor, which had been so unfortunate on the Solent. After arriving in New York on August 11, aboard the steamship *Olympic*, she was transported to Detroit, the heart of Gar Wood's territorial waters.

In response to the British boat's four Sunbeam engines, which boasted some 2000hp, Gar Wood launched *Miss America II*. He took four Liberty V12 engines from his stock to provide about 1800hp. He enjoyed careful preparation and always took challenges from his adversaries seriously. So he was dismayed to see the beautifully-made wooden hull of *Maple Leaf VII* give way shortly after the start. *Miss America I* and *Miss America II* were able to finish the race in the order that suited them. Gar Wood consoled himself that he had overestimated the British and attained a speed of 80.56mph over the mile with his new *Miss America*.

Thereafter no-one dared to challenge him until 1926. In *The Motor Boat*, the boat designer George Crouch had this to say of Gar Wood's victories in the 1920 and 1921 British International Trophy events: *"In my opinion,* Miss America *is the fastest machine in her category ever put on the water. She took the trophy back from the British with insolent ease. Back in America, she won the Gold Cup with no more opposition. Yet* Miss America *has no new features in her design or equip-*

John Hacker was one of the great American speedboat pioneers. Among his ideas was the layout of runabouts with their controls in the forward cockpit. He designed an incredible number of winners in the major competition categories, and his designs were inspirational for boat builders the world over.

He was an inspired creator but a poor businessman, quite unlike his youthful friend Henry Ford. John Hacker's life was linked with a succession of boatyards where he knew more bad times than good ones. However his eye for a line was never affected and was always innovative and elegant.

45

This John Hacker design had an exceptionally long career. It was built in 1922 to take part in the Gold Cup under the name *Miss Mary.* Ten years later, it was adapted to the new rules and renamed *El Lagarto,* and went on to win the cup for which it had been designed on three successive occasions in 1933, 1934 and 1935.

This picture shows it in 1932 during the President's Cup race, when it raced under number G18. Its lines were copied for the boat Happy Times, which raced as number G11.

The cockpit of *Happy Times* shows the sober elegance of racing runabouts in the 1920s and 1930s.

In the center of the instrument panel, the rev counter is flanked by the absolute minimum of other dials.

46

ment but is incontestably the most advanced stage of the hydroplane's development."

Soon, however, designers and builders would find themselves in the midst of a pitiless fight which owed nothing to sport.

A RICH NEW FORM OF COMPETITION: SMUGGLING

In America, a Puritanical law which had been approved several years earlier was enforced in 1920. The Prohibition Law had its origin during wartime: an alcohol-free America was expected to consume less grain during the conflict. The defenders of the project also believed it would have the advantage of fielding contingents of soldiers and workmen whose sobriety was unquestioned. Even though the New World was devoted to its crusade for freedom and universal peace, the law was quite well tolerated.

But attitudes changed quickly. Hollywood fanned the flames of a new fire in front of an audience which continually demanded more adventure, more exoticism and more pleasures of the flesh. The time of bathing beauties, drug traffickers and bad manners was not far off. Secret drinking dens rose up like mushrooms in caves and it quickly became apparent that the law was impossible to enforce; racketeering and smuggling became prosperous activities, and gangsters built their own empires. Smugglers discovered the joy of racing speedboats at the wheel of runabouts and fast launches stuffed to the gunwales with the police in

hot pursuit. The various water frontiers in the country became the site of races, often held at night, where speed counted for thousands of dollars when a delivery would be made or intercepted.

So would speedboat racing be the precursor of fashions and changes in society? While Gar Wood and his like had been piloting their *Miss* this and their *Baby* that for several years, it was not until 1921 that Atlantic City ran a contest for scantily-dressed young ladies for the title of Miss America. In the beginning, this was just an idea dreamed up by a few local promoters and journalists to keep tourists a little longer in their hotels, but the contest went on to become immensely popular because it promised instant celebrity to some unknown, pretty young girl. Not everybody approved of this exhibition, however, and the *New York Times* was not slow to denounce the precarious morals which led young girls to parade in swimming costumes in front of an all-male team of judges. Critics also saw in it the disintegration of fundamental social values, because it offered a reward for talents which had nothing to do with work or sacrifice.

JOHN HACKER, A GREAT PIONEER

John Hacker was born in 1877. From the age of fourteen he was fascinated by building model boats. Living in Detroit in an environment which particularly favored the development

The characteristic rudder mounting of *Happy Times*, well aft of the flat stern with its twin exhaust outlets.

This reproduction of the lines of the Gold Cup triple winner shows the greatness of John Hacker's timeless talent.

It is seen here carrying one of the racing numbers used in its career. This 26 feet runabout is always a great success on its rare appearances.

of his mechanical interests, he spent the best part of his youth between his job in an engine workshop and stretches of water where he tried out his own machines. A young employee called Henry Ford was working hard for the same firm and spent all his free time perfecting a small car.

The two pioneers became friends, but they were very different. Ford had business sense and went on to build an industrial empire. Hacker was an artist whose passion for boats led him to become involved in business, but he had great difficulty keeping his place in business because of his fragile health. The Hacker Boat Company and all his other companies changed hands frequently, even though they had at their disposal one of the greatest talents of the first half of the century.

John Hacker was an intuitive and daring man of ideas, and together with George Crouch and Chris Smith he was one of the innovators who achieved an incredible number of victories between about 1910 and 1939. In fact, John Hacker did even better than his peers in terms of longevity, and achieved a unique feat in the annals of motor boat racing history. For the 1922 Gold Cup, he designed a runabout with very pure lines called *Miss Mary*. This boat would go

on to have the longest top-class sporting career ever achieved by a racer. Modified several times to take account of changes in the rules, this Hacker design was renamed *El Lagarto* and went on to win the Gold Cup on three successive occasions—in 1933, 1934 and 1935—more than ten years after she was built.

The three designers listed above were largely responsible for the progress made with planing hulls after about 1910. But Hacker was a more prolific ideas man than the other two: every year he built or had built several successful boats; he was also one of the very first to publish designs, which were a factor in his widespread and lasting reputation. But in so doing he became a source of inspiration for his rivals, and Hacker, synonymous with speed and elegance, was often copied. He is credited with designing the first runabout with its cockpit placed forward, built in 1916. This new style would go on to become obligatory a few years later for all the runabouts which came out of the post-war boom. The same thing happened throughout Hacker's life: his ideas generally did much more for other people than they did for him.

In this connection the story of the Belle Isle Boat and Engine Company is typical. The company started its career

Arab VI was based on a 1922 Hacker design which was published a year later. The original boat, which carried the racing number G3 (Gold Cup category), finished second in 1922 behind Jesse Vincent's *Packard Chris-Craft*.

That year restrictions were placed on the competitors for the first time. The new rules were salutary for some and too prudent for others, but they gave rise to some marvelous runabouts which could also be used outside racing.

48

Beginning in 1922, competitors in class G started to use runabouts with racing crews of two, but the rules demanded that they had to have two additional places which could be used for pleasure boating. *Boat builders could put the four places in one or two cockpits. In 1922 and 1923, they tended to put the crew and passengers together behind the engine.*

by buying four Hacker runabouts without engines. These excellent boats, equipped with 125hp Hall Scott engines, were shown under a new name at the New York Boat Show in 1920. Christened Belle Isle, the name of a large island in the Detroit river, these first models inspired a range which became more and more appreciated: the runabout with its cockpit forward, for four or more people, was established for good. The fashion for the American speedboat—standardized, fast and comfortable—was born, and several makes would join the fray in both the commercial and sporting fields. John Hacker, the man who started it all, produced just a few examples every year, and they won their fame in the new competitions reserved for gentlemen.

CORRECT MANNERS WAS EXPECTED

After the arrival of planing hulls in the second decade of the century, the boats which dominated the great American competitions became less and less civilized. Little flat hulls, virtually without decks, were fitted with enormous engines whose exhausts vented their burning gases a few inches from the crews. These racers exceeded 60mph, then 75mph and even 80mph thanks to their war-surplus aero engines.

Yet these monstrous and extremely rapid boats did not last very long; and so the idea of competitions reserved for more sober boats gradually took hold. It was while waiting for the start of a Gold Cup heat in 1918, postponed because the weather had made the surface of the water impractical for stepped-hull hydroplanes, that Carl Fisher had the idea

of creating a new racing class. He was the owner of the Indianapolis racetrack as well as a speedboat enthusiast, and he wanted to see the evolution of real boats which could actually be used after racing.

The first Fisher-Allison Trophy race was held in 1920, and was won by *Rainbow I,* a boat designed by George Crouch which beat John Hacker's *Adieu.* The new regulations left designers enough room to dream up some marvelous machines. Cylinder capacity was limited to 1500ci, and hulls had to be at least 32 feet long. Transmission was direct, without a reverse gear. But the most interesting point was that races had to be run, regardless of the weath-

Baby Sure Cure **was the opposite of what was known as a gentleman's boat.** *Its V12 Liberty engine, clearly visible here, gave it high performance but its wild handling was characteristic of certain categories of boat built without restrictions. These were forbidden by new rules introduced in 1922.*

er conditions; judges were no longer allowed to postpone a race. So the boats conceived to meet these regulations had to be stronger, more reliable and more seaworthy.

Carl Fisher's initiative set off a new train of thought about the value and practice of motor boat racing, and went on to have a major influence on the evolution of the sport. The 1921 Gold Cup was the last one to be run under the old rules, without restrictions. The competition world was hopeful of shaking off the constant domination of Gar Wood, apparently founded uniquely on the power of his engines, and there was a radical change in the rules for the 1922 Gold Cup: stepped hulls were banned, boats had to be at least 25 feet long, and engine capacity was limited to 625ci. This marked the end of the extravagances ushered in with the arrival of Liberty engines; now, the future belonged to slower boats which were assumed to be safer.

The number of participants in the 1922 event suggested that the sporting authorities had got it right. The most powerful boat present had just 200bhp, from a Liberty engine cut in half, whereas 900bhp had not been uncommon a year earlier. The winner was a sprightly Colonel Vincent, in his 185bhp *Packard Chris-Craft*, and the winning speed fell from 1921's 69.6mph to just 40.4mph in 1922. Ironically,

Signaling with placards during the 1920 Gold Cup in Detroit.
By this stage, effective communication was becoming established between those on shore and the boat crews.

Once standardized runabouts entered series production, the competitions organized for them gave rise to some enjoyable events on the water.
This picture was taken at Detroit in 1923, and shows various products of Belle Isle Boats and their elegant crews. The boats all had Hall-Scott engines.

Colonel Vincent was none other than Jesse Vincent, designer of the Liberty V12 engine which had unwittingly caused so much trouble since its appearance in 1918. The year of his success was the first year his engine was no longer eligible for the event.

The Fisher-Allison Trophy had opened the way for restrictive regulations, but it now lost its interest and disappeared. But speedboat racing, especially in the United States, was not just about major events, and the sport's vitality could be measured by the number of competitors who could be gathered together for local races with small and inexpensive boats. The role played by the Mississippi Power Boat Association was a good example of this. The classes defined by this association of clubs were based on the most common engine sizes for motor cars and volume-produced aircraft—which kept costs down. The resulting events were wide open, and often exciting. The smallest category was defined as 151ci, and for this Chris Smith designed a small hydroplane called *Margaret III*, which was just 16 feet long and had astoundingly good handling: at a speed of 30mph, it could turn through 180 degrees in less than its own length. The speeds achieved in popular events began to get closer to those set by the professionals in major competitions.

The Hall-Scott engines stand at the 1920 National Boat Show in New York unostentatiously displayed an aero engine alongside others intended for boats.

This sea-sled was perfectly happy out at sea, unlike the classic runabouts of the 1920s. Designed by Alfred Hickman, it anticipated the development of catamaran applications for ocean navigation. *Alfred Hickman put forward a number of new ideas after about 1910, among them the semi-submerged propeller. His technical achievements were remarkable, but he was unable to turn them into good business.*

Godfather VI was the sixth boat built in 1922 by Chris Smith's new boatyard, which operated under the Chris-Craft name.

Seen here is the original boat, fully restored with its 90bhp V8 Curtiss OX5 engine.

In 1923, George Crouch summarized the evolving situation in these words: *"The 1920s marked the beginning of a period of restrictions. Limits were set on all aspects of competition: hull, engine, transmission, race distance and course conditions. In the past, size restrictions had generally been imposed by the designers, whereas today they are set by the owners and pilots of the boats themselves. In other words, the competitors choose the practical aspects they prefer rather than finding themselves trapped in a class defined solely by mathematical boundaries. A lot of effort is made to ensure that races are a real test of the qualities of this or that type of boat. If the important issue is the boat's maneuverability and its ability to turn in a short distance, trials are organized over a short distance, with a high number of laps and tight turns. If reliability is being tested, the engines are sealed throughout the event. In every case, the trial is designed to test the qualities sought in the boats, and no complicated formula is needed to do that. This new way of thinking is gaining ground at the moment, and it is an extremely important thing for motor boat racing. It will revitalize the sport."*

And, of course, some of the most experienced boat-builders would derive maximum profit from the new era which was beginning.

THE MAHOGANY EMPIRE OF CHRIS-CRAFT

Boat-building was a family affair for the Smiths. Father Chris created hydroplanes which racked up victories for a decade or more, and he was surrounded by his children whose different skills guaranteed an unbroken dominance of most waters used for racing. Jay was considered to be the best mechanic and co-pilot in the United States, and his knowledge of marine transmissions and power units was widely respected in racing circles. Bernard was also an exceptional mechanic, and the two younger sons, Owen and Hamilton, worked in the boatyard while their sister Catherine kept the books. They made a remarkable and disciplined team which worked hard and well together.

Chris Smith's main activity was racing and, after 1917, he linked up with his best client, Garfield Wood. Smith's ingenuity and Wood's insatiable appetite for winning quickly resulted in the first generation of *Miss America* boats, which won the two most coveted trophies in the world for the Detroit millionaire.

After their successful defense of the Harmsworth Trophy in 1921, a few cracks appeared in the relationship between Chris Smith and Gar Wood. *Miss America II* became their last joint success. From this point on, Smith made clear that he wanted his independence and, as the first man to exceed the 50, 60, 75, and 80mph barriers, he already had an extraordinary reputation. As most of his small boatyard was retained by Gar Wood, Wood's competition boats took absolute priority over all other projects. But when Chris Smith found a little time, he built his own boats—in particular a runabout which he displayed at the 1920 New York Boat Show. This was the 28 feet *Miss Nassau*, one of the first and possibly the very first runabout to be powered by a Liberty engine.

After 1922, the conflict between Gar Wood's competition needs and Chris Smith's wish to get involved in the expanding runabout market became too great. Smith's team became independent once again in February 1922 under the name of the CC Smith Boat and Engine Company. The first *Chris-Craft* was a 26-foot boat, available with single or twin cockpits and powered by a four-cylinder Hall-Scott aero engine.

Jeff Rodengen's book, *The Legend of Chris-Craft*, makes clear that production increased greatly during the first two years of the independent boatyard's existence. Twenty-four motor boats were delivered in 1922, and 33 the following year. The most famous motor boat marque of them all, born out of top-class competition, was about to conquer the world.

EUROPE IN SEARCH OF NEW FRONTIERS

There was a moroseness about European events which stood in marked contrast to the gaiety seen on American waters. Yet the idea of new and less extreme classes developed at the same time on both sides of the Atlantic. The loss of interest in major events held on the Old Continent was alarming. The Americans wanted to use their leisure-boats

Chris Smith's numerous competition victories assured the success of his boatyard, but he always liked to give the impression of being a simple man with down-to-earth values.
He is pictured in 1923 working in the fields, smoking one of the cheap cigars he always affected.

The restoration of the *Godfather VI* is particularly well done, as evidenced by the more-than comfortable leather-seats

The pilot's seat shows the manufacturer's plaque from Chris-Craft. On the steering wheel, two levers control the throttle and the spark advance.

for racing, while in Europe there was not enough of a leisure element in the speedboat scene. From these two different causes came the same ideas, if not actually the same effect.

In its report on the Monaco Meeting in April 1922, *Le Yacht* magazine indulged in a rousing plea for speedboat racing to embrace boats which could actually be used: *"The value of high-speed events cannot be doubted, as these play their part in developing the power and durability of engines as well as in developing shapes best suited to counter the drag of the water. Nevertheless, we would like to see awards and prizes of increasingly high value given for qualities of endurance in motor boats used in poor weather conditions. Then we will no longer see events postponed on days when sailors would describe the sea as calm, simply because some amazing racing machines are too fragile to survive the slightest swell. It is not possible to calm the sea to suit the inventors of boats designed to skim along its surface, so we should build boats which are properly suited to the job in the sort of conditions which occur most frequently."*

That year, the results at Monaco showed that the unrestricted racers had probably reached a dead end, even though they had been well adapted technically to the tough sailing conditions of the Mediterranean. There were strikingly few foreign entrants, although the Italians did muster a few as a neighborly gesture, and the lack of any British or American boats virtually undermined the meeting's credibility. It is difficult to draw any general conclusion from the Monaco results; the fact was that there were several races, several prizes and several classes, but that all of them harked back to a time when the only people who came to watch the motor boat races in the Principality were an industrial and financial elite.

Just as a horserace-goer might imagine events which cheerfully mingled galloping, a harnessed trot, steeplechase, jumps, a harness concours, and so on, so *Le Yacht* subtly redressed the balance by putting in a good word for top-class competition boats shortly afterwards: *"The sight of competitors racing across the water at top speed amidst the elegant swirl of white waves does excite the public, and in particular today's youth with its fascination for speed. To this spectacle, we owe several features of our best racers, among them multiple-skinned hulls, light and supple ribs, flat arches, stepped hulls and keel shapes which have since been used in the construction of large destroyers and fast reconnaissance cruisers. We would like to hope that a challenge will be issued to foreign nations so that the world water speed record can be disputed next year on the incomparable course off the shore of Monte Carlo.. As soon as the present economic crisis abates*

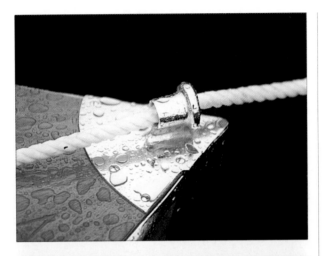

Godfather VI is one of three rare existing examples of the first runabouts. It demonstrates with elegance the simplicity with which the builders of the 1920s blended form and function.

The joy of speed aboard a gentleman's runabout from 1923.
Both pilot and mechanic sit in a cockpit similar to that of a racing car. Baby Jane was pictured here at around 60mph during a heat of the Gold Cup.

enough to lower the cost of hulls and engines and allow boat-building activity to begin again, there is no doubt that the Meeting will regain all the vitality it had in its first years."

In June 1922, Morton Smart, Commodore of the British Motor Boat Club, wrote: *"This is the first year since the sport began that no British owner has taken part in the great Monaco meeting. Moreover, neither France nor Great Britain issued a challenge for the British International Trophy. These two facts seem to me to indicate the stagnation of motor boat sport at present. I am convinced that the time is right to make a serious effort to give the sport back its former vitality, while bearing in mind the new economic and other conditions which have resulted from the war."* To achieve this, Morton Smart recommended the creation of an international association or the re-establishment of the Association Internationale de Yachting Automobile, to which the principal European countries had been affiliated before the war. And in the same spirit, the daily paper *Le Journal* announced on July 14, 1922 that a meeting of motor boats was being organized on the Rhine. Once again, the short list of entries included no major novelties and so demonstrated the lack of creativity on the European speedboat scene after the war. But a new initiative was about to make a profound difference.

THE LEAGUE OF NATIONS CREATES SOME RIVALRY

Monsieur Pierrard, the President of the Belgian Yachting Federation, organized an international conference in Brussels on September 27, 1922, in order to establish a new international federation. The conference was held in the marble room of the Palais des Académies. Sixteen nations had been invited, and among the ten who sent representatives were Spain, Ireland, Norway, the Netherlands, Sweden and Monaco. Italy, then in the process of turning Fascist, was absent. The United States, disinclined to get involved with a movement it could not control completely, put in Great Britain as its representative. Brussels was chosen as the seat of the new Union of International Motorboating and a vice-presidency was offered to the United States through its British delegate. Two categories were established, based exclusively on engine capacity: one was of 183ci and the other a more economical 91ci.

The conference's report showed that it was trying to exert an influence on speedboat racing worldwide: *"The study of international events like the British International Trophy and the Gold Cup of America, and the restrictions to be placed upon these challenges, were adopted by nine votes to seven. The result of this vote will be communicated to*

Miss Severn is a reproduction of a Hacker design dating from 1922. The creations of this prolific designer were widely distributed in their day and a number of new examples were built more than 70 years after their first appearance.

In the beginning, this boat could have been fitted with a 650hp Curtiss Conqueror V12 engine. Today, it has a prestigious Rolls-Royce V12, specially marinized in the New England.

Low revs, high torque and high power are united here, reproducing the characteristics sought after at the time which were the reason why big aero engines were used.

The vitality of the American speedboat scene after the war was in stark contrast to the difficulties which afflicted its European counterpart. The competitions organized in Europe during the 1920s attracted varied entries, with few new boats.

It was a French idea to hold an international meeting on the Rhine in 1923, and it was staged symbolically on July 14. In this picture, note the presence of hydrosliders—a peculiarity of European meetings—which were given their own special class.

America." It was a communication which had little effect on those who held these two events, but in Europe during the winter of 1922-23, the creation of this new 91ci category gave boatbuilding activity something of a new lease of life. The traditional April opening of the racing season in Monaco was eagerly awaited, and a special handicap race was set up there for these new boats. The boat built by the de Coninck boat-yard of Maisons-Laffitte turned in some good performances with its Amilcar engine, well below the capacity limit, but it was the Fiat-engined *Baglietto* which won the day.

As for the Monaco Cup itself, that was reserved for racers in the unrestricted class. Just five boats finished out of the eight starters, and several competitors arrived too late to pre-pare their boats properly. The main race was initially between the *Excelsior Breguet* and the Hieronymus-engined *Vienna*. The *Excelsior Breguet* was a large and solidly constructed boat built at Amphion, near Evian. It was built without a stepped

hull and had been very much designed for sea conditions. Power came from two Breguet 16-cylinder aero engines of 500hp each. However, the eventual winner—despite a late start—was the *Coq Hardi* belonging to Monsieur Jacques Menier, with two 450hp Renault aero engines in a hull built by Janin and Company. It appears not have been performing at its best, as the result of insufficient preparation.

In June 1923, the American magazine *Power Boating* published an article by T. D. Wynn Weston, who had been at the event. He wrote, *"Many of my American friends have said to me that the Monaco meeting is of little interest because of the low speeds attained there. It is important to remember, of course, that the sailing conditions there are very different from those in our events. So the designers and boatbuilders have to sacrifice speed in the interests of dura-bility and seaworthiness. Monaco is like a steeplechase; no records have been broken here, and I must admit that*

The Exclesior Breguet and Monsieur Jacques Menier's Coq Hardi (seen here) were the most powerful entries in the 1923 Monaco meeting. Boats like this one—powered by two 450hp V12 Renault aero engines—were primarily designed for difficult conditions and were not capable of very high speeds.

For 1923, boats like this were isolated and appeared only rarely at European meetings. Despite her respectable power output, she would not have had the slightest chance of winning a great international competition like the Harmsworth Trophy, which had been held since 1921 by Miss America II, *with more than 1800hp.*

Running Wild is a rare survivor of the great Liberty V12-powered runabouts of the 1920s. This 31.5 feet boat, built by Stanley on the Saint Lawrence in the northeast of New York State, had huge reserves of power thanks to its 650ci and 450hp.

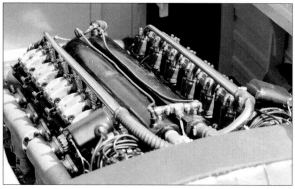

there is not a single boat here which would have the slightest chance of winning the Harmsworth Trophy. The most powerful entry, the Coq Hardi, *has two Renault 500hp engines, and if anyone suggested throwing down the gauntlet with that sort of power, I would tell him straight away that he was wasting his time]. The* Coq Hardi *was totally unprepared when she arrived in Monaco and had to be worked on round the clock at the quayside. That is not the way to win races, and the sight of it is in striking contrast to what I have seen in Britain for the Harmsworth events."*

The small racer categories raised hopes of a European revival in the midst of a very unstable international situation. Germany was bankrupt and suffering from uncontrollable inflation, strikes and poverty. French and Belgian troops had occupied the Ruhr and taken over the coal trains blocked by German railway workers, and the whole episode was punctuated by serious incidents which played into the hands of subversive communist and nationalist movements. In Munich on November 8 Hitler attempted a putsch and failed. The economic crisis reached its lowest point when the German Mark was valued at 4 billion 200 million to the dollar. Meanwhile in the United States, the dollar ruled and sport became a spectacle.

SPORT, MONEY, AND GLORY

After 1923, limits were imposed on the Gold Cup, the great annual speedboat contest. The era of the gentleman's runabout had begun. These boats were slower and more sensible than the monstrous machines which had disappeared in 1922, and their owners were supposed to be able to use them for purposes other than racing. But there were some pilots who had become used to high speeds and were not prepared to take things more slowly with restricted machines. A small group in Detroit had become very attached to the exploits of the Liberty engines which Gar Wood had so often taken to victory, and came up with a new formula called the Sweepstake, which favored large aero engines and boats over 32 feet in length.

The first Sweepstake event was organized on September 3 1923, straight after the Gold Cup. In order to attract the largest possible number of spectators, the formula was kept simple: a single heat of 150 miles, large and powerful boats,

Speedboat competitions were very popular. The Americans loved to watch sporting machinery in action, and events were organized to provide the best possible spectacle.

The great speedboat races attracted as many as 500,000 standing spectators, most of whom paid nothing for the privilege. This picture was taken at Oshkosh, where 15,000 spectators paid to sit in the stands.

and some attractive cash prizes. *The Motor Boat* magazine reported that, *"The race was merciless. Both professional reputations and money were at stake, and the unfortunate end of this event was an almost logical conclusion. Regardless of ethical considerations, I believe that money has ruined all our sports. Baseball, boxing, horse-racing and even Varsity football were all purely amateur sports in the beginning, but have now reached a stage where the pure joy of competing and the healthy stimulation of victory have been swamped by the false values of increasing wealth and of the rowdy publicity which goes with it."*

A second journalist writing for the same magazine went one better. He wrote, *"Twenty-five thousand dollars gathered by public subscription—or so we are told. [. . .] And Detroit's great respect for money is by no means an isolated case. In fact, it is entirely typical of our society. It seems highly possible that we Americans have lost the deep sense of the importance of doing things for nothing, for amusement—if we ever had it at all. The man who said that we knew the price of everything and the value of nothing really hit the nail on the head."*

It was this 1923 Sweepstake which marked the breakdown of relations between Chris Smith and Gar Wood, who had opened his own boatyard. This constructed a pair of identical new boats, named *Teddy* and *Bruin* after the furry teddy-bear mascots which each one carried. Both were very similar in design to *Miss America*, although they did not have stepped hulls; and they naturally had V12 Liberty engines. They had nothing in common with the runabouts built to meet the new Gold Cup regulations, but harked back to the period of the outrageous hydroplanes built immediately after the war. Both of them gave the impression of being built too lightly to withstand the very long distance of the race.

Bruin did encounter problems during trials, when her hull—made of two layers of thin planking, split open in several places. The aluminum reinforcing plates came away shortly after the start and completely wrecked the propeller. In the end, *Teddy* was declared the winner at the checkered flag, despite vehement protests from second-placed Colonel Vincent in the *Chris-Craft*. In fact, *Teddy* lost her engine covers and made several laps before stopping to pick up those from her abandoned sister craft. This seemed quite clearly against the rules but, in the general confusion, *Teddy* was declared the winner. This victory by a boat from the Gar Wood stable, with the help of the rest of his team, left a bitter taste in the mouths of some competitors. And this was just the beginning of the tricky relationship which would develop between the speedboat community and the Wood clan, who were set on total domination at Detroit.

The Gold Cup took place in calmer waters, among gentlemen. Colonel Jesse Vincent had entrusted his *Packard Chris-Craft*, the 1922 winner, to a newcomer named Caleb Bragg. Bragg was a motor racing driver and an aviation enthusiast, and he had a major stake in the Wright company

The arrival of electric timing devices made the attribution of records and the publication of results very much more accurate.

Miss Saint Lawrence is a 35 feet runabout designed by George Crouch in 1922. She has now been restored.

Like John Hacker, Crouch was one of the great pioneers of high-performance boats and a man who worked hard to push boat development in the direction of craft which were usable outside the competitions arena.

which held the manufacturing license for Hispano-Suiza engines in the United States. He was lucky enough to win his heat on his first outing, an unexpected success which resulted from the withdrawal of Harry Greening's *Rainbow III* after it sustained slight damage. The winning boat was fitted with one of the very latest six-cylinder Packard engines.

Despite his opposition to the new restrictive regulations, Gar Wood had not been able to resist the temptation to enter, and he made the most of the opportunity to pro-

mote his new boatyard. Colonel Vincent was there, too, with his *Baby Packard,* a Hacker boat fitted with the new special six-cylinder engine. The four leaders were involved in a terrific fight when Bragg nearly capsized in a turn. It was a magnificent contest which thrilled the 400,000 spectators. Gar Wood had the satisfaction of winning the third and last heat, perhaps his very last Gold Cup victory. As for Bragg, newly enthused by speed boat racing, he promised to return the next year.

Refueling stands at the December 1923 Sweepstake in Detroit.
In the foreground is Packard Chris-Craft II, then Miss Packard *bearing the number T-30; ahead of her is an unidentified competitor and beyond is* Snapshot II. *The mechanics are at work on board the Packard Chris-Craft II; the one with white shoes sitting on the landing-stage beside the fuel drum is holding the refueling pipe. The official standing alongside number T-30 is wearing an armband. Note the variety of shapes among the boats visible here.*

Regulation and Excess— the Golden Age

—■—

A FEW SPORTSMEN FROM THE EAST COAST OF THE UNITED STATES PLEDGED TO WIN BACK THE GOLD CUP WHICH HAD BEEN LOST TEN YEARS EARLIER. THE DESIGNER WHO INTERPRETED THEIR SECRET DREAMS DREW UP SOME MAGNIFICENT AND MEMORABLE SHAPES. OTHERS PREFERRED NOT TO SUBMIT TO RULES AND SOUGHT PURE POWER. BOTH FACTIONS CREATED MARVELOUS SOUND ON THE WATER, AND THEIR MEMORY HAS COME DOWN TO US INTACT.

—■—

Baby Bootlegger and Miss Columbia are pictured here together as they would have been in 1924. They immortalize the short period of grace when designers, builders and pilots disputed the Gold Cup with great elegance.

The middle of the 1920s saw the rise of new aesthetic trends. In 1925, Paris hosted the International Exhibition of the Decorative Arts, which encapsulated the seething creativity of the times. This artistic event was like no other held since the end of the First World War and gave legitimacy to the Roaring Twenties' paradoxical taste for luxury and abstraction. The move towards simplified lines was seen not only in architecture but also in every other branch of artistic craftsmanship. Without denying the inheritance of Art Nouveau in the first years of the century, the geometrication of forms and Cubist sources of inspiration brought about a really innovative movement in which a booming industry saw itself as mediator.

The progress made with engines offered an infinite number of new discoveries; the geographic limits of the western world rolled back before the bravery of explorers and the daring of aviators; far-off colonies provided our cities with exotic colors and materials; and speed records on land and in the air were challenged with a mad abandon which kept vast crowds fascinated with an almost religious fervor. Metal and wood were forced into sublime shapes to aid in the conquest of these intangible peaks, and the frontiers of form and function were crossed over and over again.

In the name of the conquest of technical imperatives, there arose symbols of a mechanized civilization whose beauty seemed to have been dictated only by natural laws.

PILOTS IN WHITE GLOVES

Since the end of the First World War, the destinies of aviation and yachting had been intertwined, especially in the United States. It was of course certain excesses in the use of aero engines to power the Gold Cup racers which had led to a revision of the rules governing their size. Since 1922, attempts had been made to make some kind of sense of building boats for competition, in the knowledge that runabouts were able to sail even when weather conditions were bad. The issue was to reconcile the pleasure of competition at the highest level with the current practice of motor yachting; and so there grew up a generation of boats which were balanced and equipped with reasonably powerful engines. The press of the day described them as runabouts for gentlemen.

The maximum cylinder capacity of their engines was fixed at 625ci, while minimum length was 25 feet, and skimming hulls were acceptable as long as they had no appendages, no rough surfaces and no steps designed to modify their lift in the water. In order to promote the use of these boats outside competitive events, four seats had to be available—two for the pilot and the mechanic and two for hypothetical passengers in search of excitement. Although

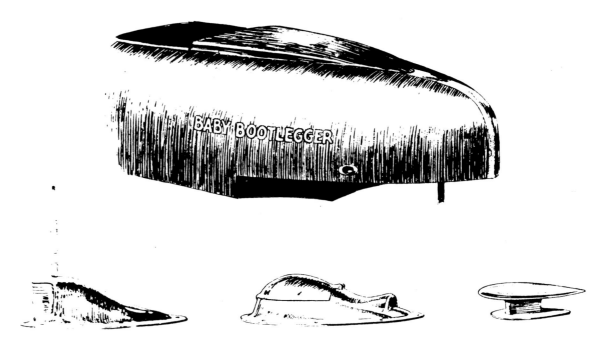

Under the influence of aerodynamics and progress in aviation, the shapes of certain objects in the motor yachting world became longer and more refined towards the middle of the 1920s.

Departing from the strict dictates of function, the purest designs were inspired by the shape of airship fuselages.

66

Skiff-shaped bodies were fitted to some highly prestigious cars in an attempt to suggest lightness, nobility and speed.
This Hispano-Suiza built for Dubonnet reflects both aircraft and boat thinking.

the boats which entered the Gold Cup in 1922 and 1923 did comply with the new regulations, they made no impact on the history of the sport, and it would be 1924 before some really memorable speedboats appeared. For a short period after that date, the elegance, refinement and performance of the Gold Cup entrants made this into a golden age which has never been surpassed.

A GOLDEN DREAM TAKES SHAPE

The Gold Cup had been traditionally held by the yachtsmen of the US East Coast, but after 1915 it was taken away by those from the Mid-West. Then, in a sign of the new times after the war, it was won by industrial Detroit, the world capital of the internal combustion engine. In September 1923, a rich New Yorker who had been a motor racing champion and a seaplane pilot struck lucky when he entered the event for the first time. Back home again, Caleb Bragg, a member of the very select Columbia Yacht Club, vowed to bring back the lost trophy.

Bragg was surrounded by yachting personalities like Charles Chapman, editor in chief of the influential *Motor Boating* review. Chapman was a well-known pilot and navigator, and he pronounced himself ready to prepare the 1924 campaign at once. The planned attack of the Columbia Yacht Club was drawn up, and at its heart was the great designer George Crouch. Crouch was a mathematics professor at the Webb Institute, who had lived in New York for several years,

The masterful creations of George Crouch reached full maturity when he designed three boats for the 1924 Gold Cup.
In a unique accomplishment in the annals of speedboat racing, Rainbow IV, Baby Bootlegger and Miss Columbia took the first three places when crossing the finish line.

and among those he had worked with had been the well-respected Nevins boatyard on City Island. Over the winter of 1923, orders flooded into Crouch's studio, among them three runabouts for the 1924 Gold Cup. The designer's capacity for work was impressive; he also had a special gift for understanding his client's wishes extremely quickly. Drawing up different boats for three different competitors in the same event with just a few weeks between them is an exercise fraught with danger. In such circumstances, creating three boats which were astonishing aesthetic, technical and sporting successes was certainly inspired genius.

THE FLOAT OF A SEAPLANE

Unlike the other two racers, *Rainbow IV* was not built in New York. The boat was ordered in autumn 1923 by Harry Greening, one of George Crouch's regular customers for whom he had already designed three *Rainbow* boats. It is clear that Crouch began by sketching the shape of *Miss*

Columbia for Charles Chapman towards the end of 1923. Shortly after that, in February 1924, he started on the design of *Baby Bootlegger* for Caleb Bragg.

From the moment it was first seen, the appearance of this boat caused a sensation, exciting both surprise and admiration for its original style and exceptional shape. George Crouch was very good at listening to his clients and translating their dreams into plans on his drawing-board. He tried to establish a close working relationship between customer and designer, and there was no doubt that the personality of Caleb Bragg could be detected in the lines of *Baby Bootlegger*. Bragg's career as a motor racing champion was cut short by the war, when he became enthusiastic about aviation. In 1917, he was sent as an attaché to the Paris Embassy, where he took part in the negotiations which led to the Wright brothers being granted a manufacturing license for the Hispano-Suiza V8 engine. After the war, he flew various aircraft when he was not sitting on the

The engine bay of *Baby Bootlegger*, pictured in 1924 and again today. She has a 625ci Hispano-Suiza V8 engine, built under license by the Wright company towards the end of the First World War. An engine of the same type has been fitted out slightly differently over the years.
The pictures show that the modern-day finish is rather neater than the original. This is also the case with other boats which still survive today.

The inscription on this cover-plate belonging to Baby Bootlegger makes a clear reference to the French engine company, whereas Wright tended to play down the origin of its products in the sporting press.

This view of *Baby Bootlegger*'s hull, looking towards the stern, reveals the great care which was put into her construction by the well-respected Nevins boatyard of City Island, New York.

The double-planking is of Honduras mahogany, 3.1mm thick inside and 6.3mm thick outside, while the keel is made of oak. The planking is held together by thousands of countersunk screws.

Board of Wright Aeronautical. The aviation world was small, and a meeting with Colonel Jesse Vincent, the Liberty engines man at Packard, led him to take an interest in the speedboat racing to which the effervescent Colonel devoted so much of his time. Bragg was a man of action, and he took a keen interest in the development of commercial seaplanes; he also broke the altitude record for two-seater seaplane in September 1919, flying from his home base at Port Washington. When his skill as a pilot was rewarded at the 1923 Gold Cup in Detroit, he decided to take the helm of his own racer. As was only to be expected, *Baby Bootlegger* was equipped with the same type of Hispano-Wright V8 as her stablemate *Miss Columbia*; the engines had been marinized by an independent company, and appeared promising.

During 1924, the Wright company took a close interest in the links between aviation and speed boats. In such a context, it is no surprise that the shape of *Baby Bootlegger* and its handling placed it at a kind of boundary between the air and the water. The boat was like the float of a mythical seaplane, skimming the emulsion it generated, and seemingly ready to defy the barriers of gravity as if in a dream.

This grand dinner at the Columbia Yacht Club in New York gathered together the principal actors in the East Coast attempt to regain the Gold Cup, nine years after its departure for Detroit.

The table has been laid to resemble the stretch of water on which the victory would be won. Among those present are several millionaires who often figured in the society pages. More familiar faces are those of Charles Chapman (nearest the camera, left), Horace Dodge (right, foreground), George Crouch (second on the right) and Caleb Bragg (fourth on the right).

Wright Aeronautical displayed *Baby Bootlegger* next to its marinized aero engines at the Motor Boat Show in New York, at the beginning of 1925.

The Gold Cup is on the foredeck of the boat, whose satin-finish varnish is much less shiny than today's equivalent. Above, the cockpit of Baby Bootlegger.

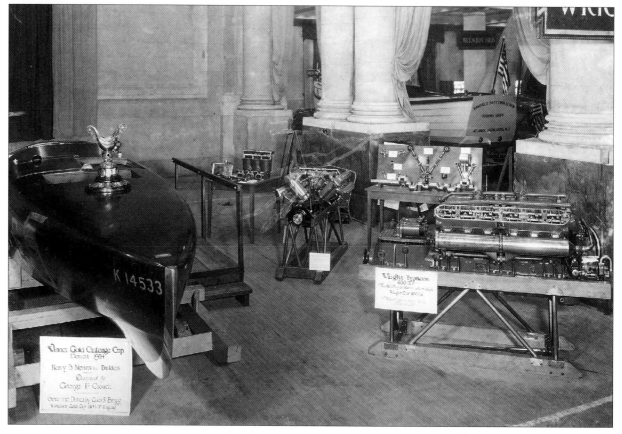

70

THE ETERNITY OF A MOMENT

The pilot slips into the cockpit with its deep cushions of green leather. In front of him is a dashboard set off by brass circles. The wide-open engine cover panels allow the polished pipes of the Hispano engine to gleam in the light. A few trickles of aviation fuel escape from this reliquary with its colors of old wine, protected by a mahogany casing.

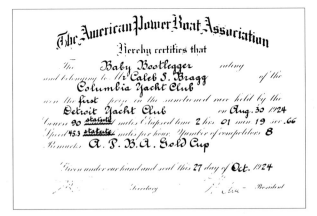

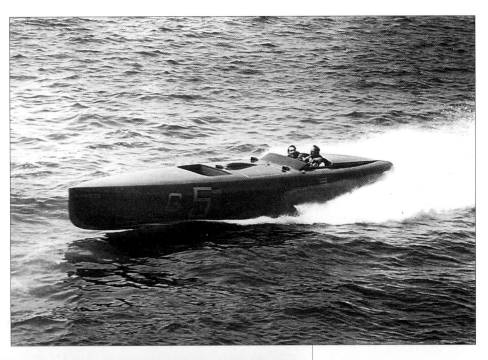

This is *Baby Bootlegger* in 1925 after being re-engined with a Packard six-cylinder.

The front cockpit is open as she thrusts through the water. Class rules demanded space for two passengers. The Gold Cup winner was awarded an official certificate recording its performance; pictured (left) is the 1924 document.

The search for *Baby Bootlegger* and the discovery of her miraculously well-preserved hull are the stuff of a true thriller.

There is something magical about the way Baby Bootlegger passes through the swell. George Crouch's lines tame the water perfectly. No other boat in this category possesses the same powerful elegance which allows her to remain flat while sailing or while turning, with neither effort nor uncouth lurches.

Enshrined in their jewel-boxes of rare metals, eight pistons fire up and begin their ritual dance with the deliberate slowness of dervishes. The clear water foams gently as it is struck by the eight regular hot breaths of the exhaust. The long foredeck with its thousand rivets stretches out towards the bow, pointing towards the horizon.

The cockpit becomes an other-worldly place, where a feeling of irresistible harmony settles between the varnished planks. Ahead, the exciting smells of the engine's furnace surround some tentative but successful attempts at combustion. To speak of speed is fruitless, for speed is obtained only at the expense of something else. But here, there is nothing of the kind: no struggle and no effort.

Baby Bootlegger does not conquer the terrain she leaves behind so rapidly; she becomes an element in the universe of movement, swifter than the liquid matter she skims yet slower than the stars she reflects. The pilot performs a few turns without interrupting the Hispano engine's song. For a moment, matter becomes heavier but the smooth keel demands more forces so gracefully that its wishes are granted at once. The curves of *Baby Bootlegger* describe every ellipse with the distant elegance of a comet. She is a masterpiece which outlines the frontiers of a better world and leaves a lasting impression of them in the memories of all those who approach her.

THE REAL BOOTLEGGING BABES

The name *Baby Bootlegger* evokes the troubled period of Prohibition during which the boat's story began. Some fertile imaginations have been quick to suggest that her speed

Rainbow IV **won the Gold Cup on the water, but was disqualified in favor of** *Baby Bootlegger.*

The hull of this runabout was recreated in its initial shape, and can be seen and admired at speed today. Note the large spray of water behind the stern and the fine bow-wave resulting from the construction of the bottom.

This detail shot of the bottom shows how the overlapped planking forms small ridges, which the Gold Cup judges considered to be a series of steps—which were illegal by this stage.

The disqualification of Rainbow IV nevertheless did not deprive George Crouch of a victory, because he designed the two boats which followed Rainbow IV in the overall classification.

and success in competition were really attributable to origins which were rather less reputable than the pure quest for the Gold Cup. Some people have even argued that this long cigar-shaped mahogany boat was actually the favorite toy of an alcohol dealer who was also a sporting enthusiast and an aesthete. They have imagined *Baby Bootlegger* surging through the water at close on 60mph, loaded with cases of adulterated whisky and piloted by its intrepid owner with one hand on the wheel and the other busily sniping at a pursuing police boat.

Such romantic visions of this pretty boat's origins have no basis in truth. The large sums of money which financed Caleb Bragg's exploits on the water did not come from clandestine

The current version of *Rainbow IV* is driven by a semi-submerged three-blade propeller. One blade can be seen here.

This innovation is said to have been invented by Alfred Hickman in 1911. Its purpose was to reduce the drag from the propeller.

Bathed in the crude light of the boatyard, *Rainbow IV* shows her robust originality, quite different from the calm balance suggested by the same year's other Gold Cup entrants.

distilleries. As a member of the society of his day, Bragg certainly did allow himself to criticize the authorities and to provoke as much as he dared. Hence the name of his boat. The term 'bootlegger' actually refers to a special method of carrying inflammable liquids which was particularly fashionable in the 1920s. In the era of Prohibition, young ladies took advantage of the prevailing fashion for long skirts and strapped flasks with a variety of contents to their legs. These precious cargoes of alcohol thus evaded the controls and checks of a Puritan America and were delivered directly, at all hours, to the places where they were to be consumed.

THE FOOT OF THE RAINBOW CROSSES THE BORDER

Rainbow IV was the fruit of a long collaboration between George Crouch and Harry Greening. They did a lot of work together to give competition boats better seagoing qualities and to make them useful outside competition. The work they did together for various trophies over many years was fundamental, and always avoided the temptation to be spectacular.

Rainbow IV **is an extraordinarily effective boat, particularly in a gentle swell.**

The multiple small steps on her hull and the semi-submerged propeller perform miracles at different angles of list.

The *Rainbow* lineage consisted of boats which were fast, strong and well protected—exactly the sort of boats to bring progress into the speedboat world. In its edition of October 18 1924, the magazine *Le Yacht* devoted a rare and detailed article to *Rainbow IV* and to competition in the United States.

"Now that the British International Trophy is a thing of the past, the most important international challenge in speedboat racing is the Gold Cup, which is run every year in Detroit, in the United States. This year's sensational event opened on September 1 and continued over the two days which followed. The new racer Rainbow IV, *owned by Mr. H. B. Greening, triumphed even more brilliantly than its predecessor* Rainbow III, *which won the cup last year and beat the 24-hour record by covering 1,064 miles at an average speed of 44.3 knots.*

"The new champion has some interesting features in its construction, and these can be seen in the photographs. The Gold Cup rules state that the overall length at the waterline should be between 25 feet and 40 feet, while the engine capacity must not exceed 620ci. Mr. Greening has used the engine from Rainbow III, *a Packard six-cylinder with a bore of 5 inch and a stroke of 5 1/4 inch, which develops around 200hp at 2000rpm.*

"The hull is tapered at each end, the stern being only 14in wide at the keel and just 5in wide at deck level. The screw is so arranged that its blades emerge from the water and its driveshaft comes right out of the water when the boat is traveling at full speed. This reduces the drag resistance to an appreciable extent. The stern-post tube is watertight at both ends, and the mainshaft in this area is lubricated by the circulation of water. The hull planking is assembled by the so-called clinker-built method, and this hull can be considered to be a hydroplane type with multiple steps. Its weight is relatively high at more than 4500lbs with the crew on board, but it is nonetheless faster than Rainbow III *which weighed 2700lbs. It has not been possible to establish whether this superior speed is due to the construction of the boat or to the propeller. Mr. Greening in fact plans to replace this by a fully-submerged propeller.*

"It has been stated that at full speed, the boat is lower at the front and skims across the water as if it were ice, probably drawing no more than 1 inch. This remarkable racer performs equally well in rough water, but when traveling slowly, the cavitation of the propeller is so great that the speed drops to eight knots at an engine speed of 800rpm. Rainbow IV *was enormously well-received throughout this season at Detroit, because it is possible to see in this boat a new type which opens broad new horizons for boatbuilders to research."*

After *Rainbow IV* claimed a clear victory in the Gold Cup and was then disqualified, her owner Harry Greening set out to break records; he wanted to prove that his racer was worthy of an unquestioned title. *Rainbow IV had a hull which was extremely rapid in all conditions; freed of class restrictions, Greening fitted it with a Liberty V12. On October 2, 1925, he broke the 24-hour distance record on a Canadian lake at a average speed of 50.78mph.*

The dashboard of the new *Rainbow IV* is very sober, even austere, in keeping with the image of this racer which was outstanding only because of her performance. Her technical innovations condemned her to a lonely existence in record-breaking.

Miss Columbia **bucks under the power of her 250hp Packard Gold Cup six-cylinder engine.**
This replica of the 1924 boat is fitted with the same type of engine as powered the original after 1925, when it replaced the original 220hp Hispano-Suiza-Wright V8.

The pointed stern of *Miss Columbia* **carries a strong-looking rudder control. All chromed fitting like these were recreated from archive photographs.**

RETURN OF THE STEPPED-HULL AFFAIR

When those lines were published, *Le Yacht* magazine was not aware that *Rainbow IV*'s victory had been the object of a protest which would later lead to her disqualification. There was great confusion in Detroit after the race was over, and those representatives of the American specialist press who were present were unable to pass on accurate information.

It was a magnificent race from start to finish. There were three heats, and three competitors stood out from the crowd in the first one on account of their speed, their regularity and the effect they had on the spectators. *Rainbow IV, Baby Bootlegger* and *Miss Columbia* finished in that order in the overall results at the end of the third heat, and *Rainbow IV*'s victory was indisputable. Henry Greening's black boat, with its distinctive hull and the huge fan of spray thrown up by its propeller, simply flew along the course.

However, the general elation which greeted the end of the race was swiftly tempered by the announcement of an objection. A competitor who never had any chance of finishing among the first three boats had made a formal protest before the race had started. So there was no question of the bitterness of defeat; instead, this protest was intended to draw the judges' attention to the illegality of the victor's hull. The Gold Cup rules stipulated that bottoms should have no steps. Most unusually for a racing boat at this level of competition, *Rainbow IV* was clinker-built, and covering one layer of planking with another—especially at the front third of the hull—had created a small series of ridges in a fan shape. The protest was based on the fact that these ridges were equivalent to a series of steps.

There was no question about the designer's intentions; he knew very well that his choice of construction would modify the behavior of the racer's bottom. Nevertheless, clinker-building had been legalized by the class regulations after 1923, and those who had drawn up the rules had probably not thought of the potential conflict with their outright ban on steps. George Crouch thought he had taken every precaution necessary when he had the boat inspected by the sport's authorities while she was under construction at the Ditchburn boatyard in Canada. No problem came up until the day of the race, when the officials took refuge behind their incompetence in matters of interpreting the rules.

So a decision was deferred for several days while the wise men of the Gold Cup conducted their deliberations.

The refined dashboard of *Miss Columbia*. This was the way her owner Charles Chapman wanted it; he was a distinguished sportsman and a great figure in American yachting.

A great day for the Columbia Yacht Club in the summer of 1924. The object of admiration is *Miss Columbia*, which carried the club's hopes of winning back the Gold Cup in Detroit.
Contemporary photographs show that the surface finish of the hull was quite different from that of the present-day boat, which has a more shiny finish and was made by different methods and with modern materials. The same can be said of several details of these modern interpretations of original boats which have now disappeared.

A moving moment: *Miss Columbia* is lowered into the water, guided by the expert hands of her builder Henry Nevins and—guiding her stern—her designer George Crouch.

The Columbia Yacht Club's new racer was very different from Crouch's other two creations for that year's event. Crouch's ability to adapt to the personality of each client was indicative of his exceptional talent.

They decided to disqualify the boat which had finished first in favor of *Baby Bootlegger*. An embarrassed press was obliged to print retractions—and a boat from New York had won back the cup after its ten-year absence.

CROUCH WAS STILL THE WINNER

The bitterness of a victory won in the committee room rather than on the water was tempered by the beauty of the boat which was declared the winner, and by the skilled piloting of Caleb Bragg, a newcomer to speedboat racing. *Miss Columbia*, placed second, reaped the reward of her balanced temperament. They say that happy people have no stories to tell. This elegant boat and her no less elegant cox, Charles Chapman, were a reminder of the restraint and discreet superiority which infused the practice of yachting in the clubs of the East Coast.

George Crouch had pulled off a remarkable feat, as the designer of all three winning boats. As for the judges, when they decreed that the clinker-built keel did not meet the rules, they took a very conservative position out of fear that extreme boats would return to their event. However, the Gold Cup was now closed to progress and had begun to lose credibility; the rules needed to evolve, and all their action achieved was to delay that evolution by a few years.

CALEB BRAGG'S REVENGE IN 1925

Caleb Bragg was not a man to be satisfied with a victory by default. So it was with some vigor that he set about defending the cup he now held, and to do it on his own territory.

Baby Bootlegger and *Miss Columbia* met again on the waters of Manhasset Bay, at Long Island, New York, on August 29 1925. Both these Columbia Yacht Club racers had been re-engined. Bragg had abandoned his Hispano-Wright V8 with some regret, in favor of a more powerful Packard Gold Cup special. This new engine was derived from Packard's V12 aero engine, and used one of its two banks of six cylinders. With a cylinder capacity of 622ci and a power output around 275hp, its construction no longer drew directly on that of the Liberty engine with its separate cylinders. The valvegear was also concealed beneath a rocker cover.

A big crowd assembled to watch these two rivals, and the 1924 winner continued to excite general admiration. More than 2,000 yachts of all sizes gathered around the course. There was unanimous praise for Bragg's skill as a pilot and for the clear victory of *Baby Bootlegger*. Observers noted the unique way she clove the swell perfectly. Nothing seemed able to slow this mahogany torpedo as she tamed the elements.

RAINBOW IV BREAKS A RECORD

Henry Greening liked to demonstrate the qualities of his boats in all conditions, and was keenly interested in long-distance record attempts. In 1925, he made an attempt on the 24-hour distance record with *Rainbow IV,* and *Le Yacht* magazine, which took a special interest in the fortunes of the black boat, reported the event in detail.

"Contrary to what one might believe, this was not a non-stop run but was done over two periods of 12 hours. In fact, the Canadian government refused permission for the run to continue through the night. They argued that an accident at such speeds could have particularly regrettable consequences, and that these would bring public discredit to an event which has an undisputed interest from both sporting and mechanical points of view.

"The run began on October 2, under the official control of the American Power Boat Association, and over a course of 19.5 miles which had been laid out on Lake Rousseau. In 12 hours, Rainbow IV covered 624 miles at an average speed of 49.93mph. The following day, she set off again at the same time (6am), and by the end of the day had taken the 24-hour distance record to 1,218.88 miles at an average speed of 50.78mph.

"For the whole of this period, the engine ran perfectly at a speed between 1800 and 1900rpm. Fuel consumption was 600 gallons, and oil consumption 15 gallons. The oil's temperature never exceeded 54 degrees, and its pressure remained constant. Refueling took place every two hours during a three-minute stop. These stops could have been shortened by using a more efficient method of refueling, and the average speed would then have increased to 52.5mph.

"Last year, the racer Rainbow IV took part successfully in the Detroit regattas. She was driven by a semi-submerged propeller which was replaced by an ordinary screw on this occasion. Her engine is of the Liberty type, modified by Gar Wood, with a 400hp output but limited to 350hp on the mainshaft. This boat can just exceed a speed of 60mph, with her engine turning at 2200rpm and her propeller at 3000rpm."

A TIME OF UNUSUAL CHALLENGES

Over the winter of 1924, 40 feet a powerful runabout by the name of *Teaser* was tested for speed on the Hudson river. The 1920s were a period which saw all kinds of attempts; speed, technology and travel captured the collective imagination. In New York, fast boats were to be seen daily on the immense stretches of water around Manhattan.

Teaser's challenge was to compete against the clock with the fastest train of her day, the *Twentieth Century* which

The Gold Cup rules were changed in 1922 in order to exclude the monster boats and to attract real gentlemen.

The pilot of Miss Columbia in this modern picture perfectly reflects the spirit of those rules.

Miss Packard **was a John Hacker design ordered for the 1924 Gold Cup and strangely fitted with a rival Hispano-Suiza-Wright engine of 220hp.**

Miss Columbia's **career did not end with the Gold Cup.**
A few years later, this New York thoroughbred turned up in Florida with a new identity.

Edsel Ford had close ties with the region. He had to swim for shore when his racer caught fire and was totally destroyed during the 1924 Detroit Sweepstake.
Henry Ford's son was very fond of speedboat racing.

linked Albany and New York. At the time, commercial aviation was beginning to expand, and the idea of this challenge was to demonstrate the power and reliability of Wright aero engines to a public fascinated by such exploits. So a large racing boat was chosen to beat the speed of a famous train which ran between two cities in a large industrial region. A very fast boat of the period could in fact travel almost as fast as a small aeroplane.

In charge of the attempt was Richard Hoyt, a New York financier who was member of the Board of the Wright company. He was a pioneer of commercial aviation, and his hope was to promote a seaplane service whose planes would take off and land close to Wall Street. Caleb Bragg, who was also a member of the Wright Board, showed his friend the lines of *Baby Bootlegger*, and Hoyt decided to place an order with George Crouch immediately. This order was for a lengthened version of the same design, to be fitted with a Wright Aviation "Typhoon" engine of 1950ci

capacity and 625hp output. The first sketch for *Teaser* was done in February 1924, and the construction of this beautiful monster was entrusted to the Nevins boatyard.

George Crouch knew that this was a particularly creative period for him. Thirty years later, just before he retired, he decided to leave all his plans behind and gave them to a friend. Before he left his studio for the last time, Crouch gave his friend a large bundle of design drawings held together by a red ribbon, and instructed him, "If you need to get rid of all my papers one day, please get rid of these last of all." The bundle consisted of the drawings for *Baby Bootlegger* and *Teaser*.

As if on Rails

The challenge was prepared with deadly seriousness, and the course chosen makes clear that Hoyt was after a demonstration which was spectacular but had no useless artifice about it. The course covered large parts of the gigantic

Hudson river, and ran for 130 miles between New York and Albany, further up-river. The railway line followed the river closely for a large part of this distance, and the boat would be running against the current. The challenge was postponed twice during the hard New York winter of 1924 because of floating ice coming down from the north.

At last, early in the morning of May 20 1925, it was time for the off, and the sound of *Teaser*'s V12 rang out alongside a pontoon belonging to the Columbia Yacht Club. In the front cockpit, the crew consisted of Jackson Mead and Charles Chapman. Mead was the Chief Engineer of the Wright company and had been responsible for preparing the Typhoon engine, while Chapman was the editor-in-chief of *Motor Boating* magazine.

Despite the long wait for the best conditions, fog and flotsam still made sailing dangerous. The boat covered the distance in two hours and 40 minutes, its engine running at 2100rpm without the slightest problem. The train took its regular timetabled three hours and ten minutes, and was thus well beaten. *Teaser* was warmly welcomed at Albany by thousands of spectators, while factory sirens sounded and church bells rang in the morning to salute the heroes of the hour.

FORD RELEASES A TYPHOON

Caleb Bragg and Richard Hoyt were well acquainted with Henry Ford's son Edsel, who took part in many speedboat competitions. Ford wanted to buy *Teaser* and use it as his everyday transport to and from his father's factories. However, an expert's report on the hull revealed a number of significant weaknesses, because the big runabout had already taken part in several trials without an overhaul. So

Typhoon cruises rapidly on a New England lake. This new runabout is a slightly smaller version of the 1924 original, which was 40 feet long.

A few modifications had to be made to George Crouch's plans to allow the construction of a boat which was already considered ambitious at the time of her conception.

81

It has been said that *Typhoon* was an enlarged version of *Baby Bootlegger*. That is true to the extent that *Teaser,* the boat which inspired *Typhoon,* was ordered from George Crouch after sight of his plans for *Baby Bootlegger,* which he was just finishing.

Ford decided to ask George Crouch to design a sister-ship and to supervise her construction.

So was born *Typhoon,* launched in 1929. This powerful runabout made the daily round trip between the Ford property on Lake Saint Clair and the gigantic factory on Rouge River. Henry and Edsel Ford were both great lovers of fast boats, which they kept in a luxurious boathouse. But the younger Ford suffered from ill health, and his doctors strongly recommended some form of transport other than one of his boats driven at nearly 60mph. Edsel, whose time was now short, made as if to sell *Typhoon* by taking out a single small advertisement. When he died, it was Henry who disposed of the boat, which went on to change hands regularly.

Typhoon became an essential but transitory possession for eccentric millionaires, and was fitted with a variety of different engines according to the fashion of the day. She even had surplus World War II engines in the shape of an enormous Allison V12 aero engine and the Packard engine from a patrol boat. *Typhoon* made a last appearance in the specialist press when *Motor Boating* magazine told the story of a rescue attempt by a group of enthusiasts. But saving this tired Leviathan proved too much in the end; she was destroyed in a boatyard fire in Seattle in 1968.

HIGH STAKES, FROM DETROIT TO HAVANA

Some people argue that the American taste for large cylinder capacities showed itself in the speedboat world through the systematic rejection of limitations on power. And that was why the city of Detroit, which had held the Gold Cup until 1924, drew up a racing formula which attracted devotees of

The challengers on board *Teaser*. In the cockpit is Jackson Mead, Chief Engineer of the Wright firm and the man responsible for developing the *Typhoon* engine.

Next to him, on the left, is the omnipresent Charles Chapman, who was following the event for his magazine, Motor Boating. The rear seat is occupied by a Naval Officer and a mechanic.

Teaser, which inspired the building of *Typhoon*, took part in a challenge which made the news in 1924, when she raced the fastest train of the day between Albany and New York along the Hudson river.

Typhoon's large cockpits could accommodate up to ten people.

The engine compartment is positioned centrally, and contains a 574ci Chevrolet V8 engine which delivers 600hp.

the V12 engine. This series, known as the Sweepstake, went on to become very successful after the Gold Cup went back to the East Coast.

Events of this type were organized during the speedboat meetings held in the north over the summer, and in Florida or even Cuba during the winter and spring. Gar Wood, who held an absolute speed record as well as the Harmsworth Trophy, liked to demonstrate the superiority of his Liberty engines. He won the Sweepstake of 1924 in *Miss Detroit VII*, closely followed by *Cigarette, Jr.* and by *Baby Gar IV*. The three leading boats were twice as powerful—with 500hp as against 250hp—as those which finished immediately behind them

Two racers in the powerful category of the Sweepstakes in the port of Havana, 1924.

Races were organized there at the beginning of the season every year, and were added the list of winter events which had been held in Florida.

Delphine Dodge had no intention of allowing her brother to defend the honor of their extremely wealthy family all on his own.

Her enthusiasm for speedboat racing remained undiminished for many years, and both her qualities as a pilot and her great courtesy were highly valued.

In answer to the restrictions of the Gold Cup, the Sweepstake events with their very broad rules once again allowed the Liberty V12 to be heard on the water.

Gar Wood marked out his territory as that of the fastest and most powerful boats. The last-born of his imposing stable was Miss Detroit VII, *which won the 1924 Sweepstake in Detroit.*

and had come from the Gold Cup. But these impressive figures should not be allowed to mask the relative performance of these huge machines, and a comparison of average speeds shows a smaller difference than might be imagined. The winning *Miss Detroit VII* turned in an 54.8mph best, with an average of 48.7mph for the 150 mile course. *Baby Bootlegger,* which finished fifth, posted a best speed of 745.7mph and an overall average of 43mph. The differences seem small in view of the difference between the engines.

In 1925, Packard introduced its new six-cylinder Gold Cup engine, followed closely by a twin-six version boasting 550hp. This was designed for the Detroit Sweepstake, then the primary event in the absence of the Gold Cup. It was the *Packard Chris-Craft II,* equipped with one of these engines, which won the event in the hands of the irrepressible Colonel Vincent. She finished 12 seconds ahead of Horace Dodge in *Baby Horace III,* which also had a 1280ci Packard 12-cylinder engine. The boats with smaller cylinder capacities were nevertheless not far behind.

During this period, Europe was emerging with some difficulty from a post-war time of economic and social troubles. Speedboat racing was at a low ebb, despite a few rays of hope.

Vae victis!
The rules would be applied strictly and in every case by the judges of the event.

85

Europe Attempts to Emerge from Stagnation

In this period, Europe was alone in maintaining a category specially for hydrogliders, which were favored by the lobby of builders and by colonial conquests. France held the world speed record, homologated in 1924, for the statutory kilometre traversed both ways three times non-stop, with an average of 74.9mph. More generally, however, the Union Internationale de Yachting Automobile noted sadly the disparity of the situations on opposite sides of the Atlantic. The sporting authority prepared itself to get things moving once again by promoting classes for small cylinder capacities, which had had a beneficial effect on the development of the sport in the United States. The new initiatives taken in Brussels seemed to be characterized by a desire to bring the two continents closer together. In February 1924, a statement was issued presenting the rules for the Duke of York's Trophy for motor boats. This was a competition with international heats, where the first country to win two heats won

the cup, and was run for the first time a year later. The initial plan was to run a 91ci category for the competition's first three years—a decision which took account of the situation in Europe, where only relatively accessible small-engined classes were able to attract a credible number of challengers.

A comparison of the best performances recorded in these classes shows that internationalization would favor Europe. In the 91ci category, the world record was held by the speedboat *Baglietto,* and was set at Monaco on April 30 1923 at 36.95mph. In the equivalent category in the United States, the record had been set by *Buddy* over a 2.5-mile course on July 23rd, 1923, at a speed of 30.14mph.

The year 1924 saw an encouraging number of participants in the Cannes event for speedboats and seaplanes. There was excellent competition between the French, the English, the Italians and the Spanish, which was decided in favor of the Franco-Argentine racer *Sadi I.* That amounted to no more than six competitors, but this small number was

The year 1924 was definitely a good vintage for George Crouch's creations. He designed *Baby Horace III* **for Horace Dodge, the heir who spent limitless amounts of money to satisfy his appetite for speed on the water.**

As with Baby Bootlegger, *this is the original hull which has been carefully preserved.*

Baby Horace III was designed for the Sweepstake races with their rich rewards. These were organized in Detroit for enthusiasts of powerful racers.

This boat is 26 feet long. Her original 550hp Packard 12-cylinder engine has been removed, and she now has a General Motors V8 of recent manufacture.

The position of the pilot's seat, almost on top of the stern, showed which way George Crouch's thoughts for the futuristic Gold Cup boats of the same year.

The boat's whole appearance suggests restrained power.

simply the dark before the dawn. The English prepared their boats and fine-tuned them for the elimination heats of the Duke of York's Trophy. *Miss Betty,* a Camper and Nicholson hull fitted with an Aston Martin 1.5-liter engine, seemed to have the best chance.

At the end of 1924, the Union of International Motorboating met to agree on new rules, as it did every year. France was represented by Captain Massieu, vice-president of the French Motor Boat Federation, and by Monsieur Houët, President of the Motor Boat Sporting Committee.

A Willingness to Bring the Nations Together

A statement issued by the Union showed that once again, there was an attempt to be more open towards the United States and to simplify the smallest capacity class:

"The unrestricted class for boats with 725ci engines will be the maximum power class. This is recommended for major international competitions and may be used from

The extremely utilitarian dashboard of *Baby Horace III* reflects the boat's stripped-down, almost rough-and-ready, character.

Boats in this category demonstrated an opposition to the organized and supposedly innovative Gold Cup class. Here, the designer once again shows his skill in giving this 1924 racer lines which evoke a return to the past, at a time when racing machines were usually brutal in nature.

1925, among others for the King of Belgium's Trophy. [. . .] The 3 liter (183ci) class with restrictions will finish after 1925.

"The unrestricted 1.5 liter (91ci) category was adopted for the Duke of York's Trophy, with the rider that each boat must have been constructed entirely in the country which enters it. This requirement is now modified as regards the design, the electrical equipment, the magneto, the spark plugs, the carburetor and the screw. Only the hull and the engine must have been built in the country of origin."

It was quite obvious that the authorities had eased the restrictions in order to open the small-capacity class to more competitors. The suppression of the 183ci class and the increase to 125ci were evidence of a desire to move closer to the regulations in force in the United States, where speedboat competitions were not hindered by a difficult economy. The U. I. Y. A. was trying to broaden the number of countries it represented and to become truly international by recognizing the most important of the US categories.

An early initiative assured the new supremacy of the 12-liter class, when a new prize was offered by His Majesty the King of Belgium. This was to be awarded at an international speed event which would be open to American competitors:

"It is officially announced that His Majesty the King of Belgium has graciously granted his royal patronage to offer a gold medal as the first prize in an international contest for speed on the water. This will be run during 1925 and will be for speedboats in the international 12-liter class with no restrictions on the size or shape of the hull. This international series in Europe includes the American class for engines of 725 cubic inches capacity, which is a very popular class in the United States and includes speedboats capable of over 60mph. The prize offered by His Majesty the King is not offered with the

sole aim of stimulating international sporting competition. It also has the essentially practical aim of encouraging the development of a type of ultra-fast speedboat which could be of inestimable value in the colonies and overseas, where huge fast-flowing rivers offer the best means of communication for colonial administrations, postal services and trade. The limit of 12 liters brings with it a reduction in the cost of the boat, in the hourly fuel and oil consumption, and encourages a worthwhile improvement in power output."

Notable here is the important reference to colonial expansion and to its conditions, which had no direct impact on the racers from the other side of the Atlantic. From this point on, it was possible to imagine the announcement of a new international event on the Congo river. The French prepared themselves for such an event, breaking their previous world kilometre record in 1924. They used a new Farman hydoglider, powered by a 450hp Lorraine-Dietrich engine, and achieved an average of 85.63mph.

A TRIP TO AMERICA

The 1.5 liter (91ci) international category proved to be an unqualified success for the U. I. Y. A. Its development was confirmed in the United States, where the famous Duesenberg firm announced that it would be building engines for this category of boats. Several European competitors made preparations to travel to America and take part in the 1926 competitions. There seemed to be a general awakening. In the unrestricted category, a French boatyard—Excelsior, near Evian—announced in March 1925 that it would challenge Gar Wood and take the Harmsworth Trophy off him in 1926. That looked like being the major challenge of the season to come, because no challenge had been recorded since 1921.

The 1.5-liter category was in good order at the 1925 Cannes international meeting, with 11 entrants of five different nationalities. A promising new racer called *Newg*, owned by Miss Carstairs, made her first appearance on the continent and won first prize for elegance.

So 1925 ended amid a number of encouraging signs of a revival on the international speedboat scene. At the end of the year, the U. I. Y. A. announced the first results of the King of Belgium's Prize, the great contest open all year round to encourage speed record attempts in the 12-liter class and including the American 725 cubic-inch class for Gold Cup competitors. The six best-placed contestants made clear that the 180hp Wright-Hispano-Suiza V8 was the dominant force in the United States. The first four gained their awards in American events, and the

George Crouch got to know his future patron better when he designed *Baby Horace III. Following in the footsteps of his car manufacturing family, Horace Dodge planned to start series production of runabouts, and so surrounded himself with the best advisers.*

next two were French. They owed their placings to results achieved at the Côme meeting on September 26 1925. It is worth remembering that the only countries permitted to enter the contest were those which had taken part in the 1924 Olympic Games, held in France; that no commercial advertising was permitted on the boats; and that their names were not allowed to reflect the origin of the hull, the engine, the design or of any accessory whatsoever.

The sporting authority's traditional meeting at the end of the year finished with the adoption of a few minor modifications to the rules governing cylinder capacity. From now on, there would be four categories, ranging from under 1.5 liters up to 12 liters.

GAR WOOD GOES FLAT OUT

The American Gar Wood took little notice of what was happening in Europe. He had followed the challenge from

Teaser in minute detail, and did not like the idea of being left behind when it came to speed records. He could barely tolerate the idea that a boat which had not come from his stable should reign supreme; so he kept ready two of his biggest and fastest racers while waiting for reports on his adversary's attempts to beat the train. Convinced that he could keep the situation under control with his *Baby Gar* boats, he allowed himself to be caught napping by the announcement of the performance achieved by the big Wright-engined runabout. Angrily, he took up the cudgels six days later, resolved to do better on all counts. The man was a past master at promoting himself through the press, and everything about his challenges was always spectacular.

What Gar Wood wanted was to see *Teaser* back on the water to run against himself and against the train at the same time. He told the press that he would run directly against the train and not just against the clock. Gar Wood gradually

The 1924 International meeting at Cannes was open to racers, hydroglider, and to seaplanes.

The imposing presence of some warships in the port gave a broader appeal to this new annual meeting which would replace the Monaco trials.

91

The term "Baby" was applied in this case to a boat nearly 33feet long. The *Baby Gar* series were the best from the boatyard which Gar Wood created to build his machines and exploit the prestige of his countless victories.

Gar Wood made skillful use of the press to create an image of himself as a typical American hero who embodied the values of U.S. society: work, risk, sport, and luck.

piled on the pressure, and whipped the press up to fever pitch when he announced that his challenge would be accompanied by a $25,000 bet against Richard Hoyt. He added that his boats could beat any vessel powered by a Wright engine, and announced to the world that he would go one better: he would cross the Atlantic in 48 hours during 1927, traveling from Newfoundland to Cowes at an average 60mph and refueling in mid-ocean. Hoyt did not take up the challenge, and left Wood to manipulate the daily press to his own ends.

This whole affair assumed unexpected proportions in the public imagination, and the geographical configuration made a direct contest between train and boat perfectly feasible. So the management of the New York Central railway made its own position clear in an official statement:

"In response to the publication of a statement by Garfield A. Wood that he plans to race the Twentieth Century Limited *from Albany to New York next Monday morning, the management of the railway wishes to inform the public that the train will not be attempting to race. It will run from Albany to New York according to its regular timetable [. . .] The safety and comfort of passengers being the company's principal aim, any suggestion of racing is out of the question. The running of trains is governed by very strict regulations, and no exception may be made nor shall be made."*

On May 26, 1925, Gar Wood launched two of his *Baby Gar* boats into the early morning mist. Despite the calm statement from the railway management, the express was not running to its usual timetable that day. The train left

Albany 40 minutes early and arrived in New York 30 minutes ahead of its scheduled time. The New York Central probably made this exception in order to keep its distance from the event, but Gar Wood altered his timing to suit the train.

Thousands of people were attracted by the publicity surrounding this event, and they crowded along the roads which lined the river. The train's passengers also found the operation entertaining, and this everyday trip turned into a formidable match. On board the express, they were rooting for the railway, encouraging the engine driver by voice and gesture to speed up so that he should not be left behind by the boats. Meanwhile, a large group of Gar Wood's friends

and family occupied one carriage and cheered on the boats from there.

The race was transmitted "live" on the radio, with a commentator on board a bomber aircraft flying over the Hudson. Even though the aircraft latched on to the wrong train for several minutes in the mist, it was easy enough to follow the progress of the transmission because the broadcast was perfectly audible over almost the whole of the distance. As usual, Wood knew how to raise the tension; he had chosen to pilot *Baby Gar IV* and had left *Baby Gar V* to his brother George. It appeared that the engine of *Baby Gar V* was working better, and George surged ahead.

It was one of those challenges so loved by the public of the 1920s: Gar Wood promised that he, too, would race the *Twentieth Century Limited* express train along the Hudson river.

Wood carefully whipped up enthusiasm in the press, and set two carefully-prepared Baby Gar boats against the train and against the record set by Teaser.

In mid-race, right in the middle of the immense Hudson river, Gar Wood signaled to his brother to slow down. Accompanied by the omnipresent Chapman as observer and timekeeper, by his mechanic Orlin Johnson, and by a journalist, he jumped aboard *Baby Gar V* and abandoned *Baby Gar IV* to his brother. Gar set off again at full speed but, shortly afterwards, his Liberty engine showed signs of losing power. There was a second acrobatic exchange of boats in mid-river.

Baby Gar IV took two hours, 58 minutes and 20 seconds to travel from Albany to New York. The train took three hours and ten minutes, according to official timetables. So steam had been beaten—but not *Teaser*. On his arrival, Wood announced himself proud to have beaten the train, but made no comment about being defeated by his nautical adversary. Instead, he astutely kept the tension up by announcing that he was not going to stop there: he would bring his *Miss America* boats to the Hudson, because these were the fastest speedboats in the world.

The Detroit champion's boasts were of little consequence. What mattered was that the popular imagination had been captivated, and that tales of boats continued to fascinate the public of the day.

Baby Gar IV is a replica of one of the most famous boats in Gar Wood's fleet.

In 1925, the size and power of the small series of Baby Gar boats ensured that they were reserved for an elite. A 500hp Liberty engine made this one into a prestigious boat suitable for competition or as a high-speed grand tourer.

Sleek and powerful, *Baby Gar IV*
and *Baby Gar V* wait for the
moment to begin their race against
the fastest train in the United States.
Standing on the deck, bareheaded, is
the master, Gar Wood himself. The
industrial might visible in the
background lay behind Gar Wood's
challenge and lends this scene a certain
dramatic intensity.

The Continental Drift

IN EUROPE, THE SMALL-CAPACITY CLASSES WERE THE SALVATION OF SPEEDBOAT RACING. ATTEMPTS TO UNIFY THE RACING REGULATIONS WITH THOSE OF THE UNITED STATES— THEN AT THE PEAK OF ITS ECONOMIC PROSPERITY—MET WITH SOME SUCCESS. AMERICAN AND CANDIAN RACERS COMPETED ON THE OLD CONTINENT; MISS AMERICA BOATS WERE SEEN IN VENICE. GREAT NAMES FROM THE AUTOMOBILE WORLD MET ON THE WATER TO SEEK NEW GLORY.

A large French speedboat attempts to conquer the United States. The challenge from the Excelsior France— seen here on the deck of the SS France of the French Line, which brought her to New York in 1926—was a total failure. The Americans quickly forgot it, too busy producing runabouts as if they were cars.

99

For the first time since 1921, a challenge came from Europe to the holder of that most coveted trophy, the Harmsworth. The Americans waited impatiently for more than a year for the arrival of the French challenger to their champion Gar Wood. The builder and pilot of the *Excelsior France*, T. A. Clarke, was welcomed very warmly when he arrived in New York, and then again in Detroit, where the town made him an honorary citizen and treated him like a VIP. The specialist press published descriptions of *Miss America*'s rival, which seemed to be a large and solidly built boat with a conventional hull, powered by a pair of Breguet 16-cylinder engines. The French challenger had no track record, which made it difficult to work out how good the boat really was; right from the beginning, however, she did seem to be associated with lateness. The run-off was initially scheduled for 1925, but was postponed after the boat was involved in an accident while testing on Lake Leman.

In September 1926 the date was fixed and then put off again when the French boat, which had by now arrived in Detroit, proved not to be ready. The great day finally came on September 7, 1926, and over 100,000 people crowded along the Detroit river to wait for the start, scheduled for 15.30hrs. T.A. Clarke was at the controls, but he tried in vain to start his two engines. Gar Wood had no intention of being let down at the last minute after he had waited so long for this race, and so he offered his assistance. He instructed a team of mechanics to try to get the American compressed-air bottles connected to the starter of the two Breguet engines. But it was no use, and after two fruitless hours of trying, a decision was taken to try towing the racer in the hope that the consequent rotation of the screws would start the engine. *Excelsior France* coughed, and then fired.

Miss America IV, piloted by George Wood, and *Miss America V* with Gar Wood at the controls went on the offensive from the start, which was five minutes behind schedule. It would have taken about that long for the most naïve observer to realize that the French boat did not stand a chance against the speed of the two American racers. *Excelsior France* appeared to be poorly balanced, and pitched heavily. On the first run, she achieved just 42mph, while the two *Miss America* boats ran in formation at over 60mph. As the second run was about to start, T.A. Clarke returned heartbroken to the stand,

T. A. Clarke was the pilot and the owner of the Exclesior boatyard at Amphion, near Evian. He and his wife were warmly welcomed by the Americans, who were expecting a serious challenger for the invincible Gar Wood, holder of the Harmsworth Trophy since 1920. *They were sadly disappointed by the pitiful performance turned in by the only French challenger in the unlimited capacity class. The fight they had hoped for never took place.*

and conceded victory, commenting laconically to the journalists who were present, "What's the use of carrying on?"

THE FAILURE OF THE *EXCELSIOR FRANCE*

This inglorious episode makes clear that the challenge had been badly prepared by the French. Indeed, it is hard to understand why the challenge had been made at all. American observers had visited the Monaco meeting at the beginning of the 1920s, when the event was moribund, and had taken back a pessimistic picture of the standard attained by competitors in the most powerful class, which was the only one suitable for the Harmsworth Trophy. So why did the Exclesior boatyard not send a representative to check on Gar Wood's professionalism and on the perfect balance of his hulls on the river at Detroit, where conditions were quite different from the sea at Monaco? Why had so much effort, so much time and so much money been wasted to no avail? If the hope of additional industrial and commercial exchanges with the United States was among the reasons for making the challenge, why did no-one calculate the damage which would be done by such a pitiful showing? Despite all this, certain lessons which should have been learned on that sad day in 1926 clearly were not learned.

THE SMALL CLASSES START UP AGAIN

The year 1926 marked the beginning of a general movement towards the use of car-derived engines. On both sides of the

Dr. Eugenio Etchegoin, an Argentinean national who had made his home in France, was one of the key personalities in the revival of speedboat competition in France after the middle of the 1920s.

He financed the long line of Sadi *racers, built for various international categories. They earned him a good number of awards.*

Sadi III was a racer in the international 3-12 liter class. Her hull was designed by Picker, and was fitted with a 180hp Hispano-Suiza V8 engine. On September 10, 1926, she broke the world speed record at 63.34mph.

This was the best performance recognized by the U.I.Y.A., and not the absolute speed record, which was held under an American category which had not been homologated. The lines of Sadi III (1926) and Sadi VI (1927) appear to have been inspired by the 1924 American boat, Baby Bootlegger.

Atlantic, the small capacity classes gave a new impetus to competition. There was a great deal of speedboat activity in the United States, where classes 91 and 151 for 1.5-liter and 2.5-liter engines respectively attracted a larger number of pilots. In Europe, however, the situation was quite different, because the objective was simply to save the events for boats with inboard engines. The hope was to attract new competitors by bringing down the costs of construction and maintenance, and so to revitalize craft and industry in the boatyards and the engine makers who had been hit hard by the crisis in the first half of the 1920s. In this respect, the action taken by the U.I.Y.A. was decisive. By initiating a number of contacts between Europe and the United States, it

pursued its mission of developing the sport. Among its objectives was also the eventual reclaim of authority in the sport from the Americans, whose considerable weight was matched only by their fierce independence.

The Duke of York's Trophy was created in 1924, and marked real progress in the internationalization of competition. The 1926 event promised to be an event of the highest importance, and *Le Yacht* magazine enthusiastically echoed the fact: *"The challenge limited to racers in the 1.5-liter class will bring out boats which represent the best efforts from each side of the Atlantic to develop this class, which is so interesting from the point of view of car racing.*

"The participation of Mr. Greening, the Canadian yachtsman who holds the 24 hours record, and that of Mr. Carl Fisher, who has always done well in speed events, will be enough to inspire the greatest enthusiasts of this nautical sport. It is worth noting that this challenge represents a new Anglo-American match and that, unlike the now-defunct Harmsworth Trophy, it will bring together boats of the same class."

The magazine's reference to the demise of the Harmsworth Trophy was inaccurate, although it did have some basis in reality. It was true that the major disparities between defender and challenger had reduced the interest

of the races up to this point. On the other hand, to describe the Trophy as defunct was rather hasty, and failed to take account of the challenge posed by the *Excelsior France*—which, strangely, was not mentioned once in the magazine's generally well-informed columns during the whole of 1926.

SOME FIRST-RATE COMPETITORS

Interest in the Duke of York's Trophy was heightened by the rule of national representation, which demanded preliminary heats. The British ran theirs on June 11, in front of several thousand spectators, and the loudspeakers sponsored by the *Daily Mail* announced *Newg* as the winner. In the social context of the times, it was rare to find that the owner of a boat was also its mechanic; yet that was the case with this boat, which belonged to an extremely rich young lady of 20, Miss Marion Carstairs, who rode alongside her pilot. The second British entry was called *Bulldog*.

On the French side, the choice fell upon two new boats, an encouraging sign of vitality in the all-pervading gloom. One of these was Dr. Etchegoin's *Sadi II*, which had been built by the naval boatyard at Sartrouville. The hull was the work of the Swiss designer Picker, and the boat was powered by an astonishing supercharged two-stroke Etchegoin-Cauzan engine, with four cylinders and eight horizontally-opposed pistons. With its Roots compressor this unit gave 136hp at 4400rpm on the test-bed. It was very compact thanks to its flat cylinder block and had a low center of gravity which was ideal for marine use. The idea of horizontally-opposed pistons sharing a common cylinder went back to the end of the previous century, and was then taken up by the Gobron Brillié company at the beginning of the twentieth century.

Sadi II's first outings were disappointing, but the capabilities of the engine did not seem to be suspect. The boat did not plane well, plowed heavily, and shipped a lot of water; turns could only be taken slowly because stability at the stern caused trouble. A lot of work was going to be needed if this racer was to take part in the Trophy with any chance of success.

Jean Houët's *Bambino II* was one of the new French competitors in the international 1.5-liter class. *Her hull was designed by Houët and built by de Coninck at Maisons-Lafitte. The power unit was a CIME marine engine.*

Jean Houët, pictured at the wheel of his 1.5-liter racer. The 1.5-liter class was relatively accessible, and lay at the heart of a revitalization of speedboat competition in Europe under the aegis of the U.I.Y.A. *Houët was himself one of the U.I.Y.A.'s senior figures. Houët made some notable contributions on both the sporting and technical levels in both national and international arenas; his talent also showed in a number of notable films he made on different aspects of yachting.*

103

The Duke of York's Trophy in 1926 attracted a truly international entry and was evidence of a revival in Europe.

This was a very open competition, limited to racers in the 1.5-liter category which had already been selected by their country of origin. In the picture is the German entry, Mr. Krueger's Sigrid IV.

Races for the small-capacity classes became more and more successful, especially in the United States where the boats were generally equipped with small marine engines or, more commonly, car engines.

The other French competitor seemed better prepared. Her hull behaved very well in the water, which would be a trump card if the race was difficult. *Bambino II* was owned by Jean Houët, and was built by the Coninck boatyard at Maisons-Lafitte. She rode the water much better than *Sadi II*, so much so that it was not always necessary to keep the engine covered. At full speed the boat came right out of the water, and her streamlined shape cut cleanly through the air. In Jean Houët's hands she turned impressively, and seemed to have good stability at the stern. Her CIME engine, boosted by a Cozette supercharger, had plenty of performance but had not yet been proved reliable.

Canada was nobly represented by *Rainbow V*, with an eight-cylinder Miller engine. This was the racer piloted by Mr. Greening which had been belatedly disqualified from the 1924 Gold Cup. As for Germany, her entry was the *Sigrid IV*, owned by Mr. Krueger and powered by a Mercedes engine.

The first entry by the Americans aroused great curiosity. Their competitors were Mr. Fisher's *Little Shadow* and Mr. Davis's *Dixie Flyer*. Both had lightweight hulls by the Purdy boatyard, but it was the actual conception of the boats which interested observers on both sides of the

The winner of the 1926 Duke of York's Trophy was *Newg*, owned by Miss Marion Carstairs, a wealthy 20-year-old who also served as the riding mechanic.

The boat was designed by Fred Cooper, and that year she also broke the world speed record for her class with an average 44.87mph over six timed runs. The record she broke was of 43.56mph and had been held by Woolf Barnato with Bulldog, which had both engine and hull by Brooke.

The Duke of York's Trophy was held in Great Britain. Its importance was confirmed by the presence of competitors from America and Canada.

This is Rainbow V, owned by the eclectic Harry Greening who had been the unlucky winner of the 1924 Gold Cup with Rainbow IV.

Atlantic. Their eight-cylinder Miller engines ran at a very high 6,500rpm and were connected directly to the screw. This was a first of its kind, and the loss of traction was only around 20%, which surprised a number of those who believed in big and low-revving engines. These racers also incorporated another innovation which flew in the face of custom as regards the construction of hydroplanes, and this was the use of a combined rudder and stern-post. This was an old patent, taken out by in 1910 by Fauber, who was one of the inventors of the hydroplane. Normal practice was to situate the rudder of a hydroplane under the front third of the keel.

ANOTHER BRITISH VICTORY

The first heat of the Duke of York's Trophy started on Saturday June 26th. First place went to the British boat *Newg*, and second to her compatriot *Bulldog; Dixie Flyer* came third and *Sigrid IV* finished fourth. The two French racers were not placed. *Sadi II* started well, and then turned over suddenly. Etchegoin the pilot was trapped under his boat, but managed to escape and was rescued by his mechanic who had already reached the safety boat. The official French version attributed this nasty accident to a large piece of wood floating on the water which had unbal-

Miss Daytona leads by half a length in a hotly-contested race at Palm Beach in Florida.
Races in this small-capacity class were wide open.

In this long turn, Miss Daytona shows off the splendid castings of her twin-camshaft Miller four-cylinder engine.
This effective and pretty boat is one of the very few examples of her class which have come down to us. She was restored with great care, and in place of her original engine has a Miller engine which came from a car collection in Nevada.

Dick Loynes proudly displays one of the features of his four-cylinder Miller 151 Marine Racing engine. The centrifugal compressor could be fitted or detached very easily to allow the racer to take part in two different classes.

The numerous victories won by Miss California proved very beneficial to Harry Miller's business.

anced the racer, but the strange handling of *Sadi II* on test suggests that this was not the only possible explanation. The other French competitor was Jean Houët, who lost half an hour repairing the engine of his *Bambino II,* which gave trouble from the start. His petrol tank then developed a leak, and he decided to withdraw at the end of the penultimate run. The American *Dixie Flyer* was the favorite, but her overstressed engine lost power and she had to be content with third place ahead of *Sigrid IV,* which was nevertheless all of 16 minutes behind the winner.

The second heat ended with a surprise victory by the German boat. *Newg* suffered from engine trouble and finished second after a fierce struggle to regain the lead. This made for a spectacle which delighted the spectators, as *Dixie Flyer* was forced to drop out with mechanical trouble. After this heat, Mr. Krueger was presented to the Duke of York to receive the customary congratulations, but the German champion was unable to utter a word because he had been deafened by his own engine and was visibly overcome with emotion. He was unable to speak again until much later in the evening. As the two first races had been won by different nationalities, and the rules stipulated that the winner had to win two races, a third heat had to be held.

The next day, *Newg,* with her Saunders hull and Sunbeam engine, won easily and kept the trophy for her country.

Back in France, *Bambino II* finished her first season by winning the French motor boat cup. The indefatigable Dr. Etchegoin had been unsuccessful in the small capacity classes, but took comfort in trying out his brand new boat, *Sadi III,* built for the 12-liter class. A world record seemed within

Miss California **was one of the most successful racers powered by a Miller engine.**

Harry Miller had already achieved success in motor racing when he received orders for marine engines in the 151 (2.5-liter) class during 1926. Thus was born a twin-camshaft four-cylinder with two valves per cylinder, which could be supplied with or without a centrifugal compressor. Miller was equally interested in the development of the small European 1.5-liter class in the United States, and he came up with a twin-camshaft eight-cylinder engine with two valves per cylinder and a compressor.

Miss Carstairs was pictured here at the controls of *Estelle II*, beginning tests for her challenge to win back the Harmsworth Trophy from Gar Wood.

The press took a great interest in these tests; note the photographer at the right of the picture.

his grasp and the official timekeepers were asked to be present on September 10, 1926. *Sadi III* did the three timed runs, in opposite directions, at an average of 57.2mph and thus established a new world record for the 3-12 liter class. The boat's best leg was timed at 63.34mph, which was a best performance both nationally and worldwide.

A QUESTION OF ENGINES

As we have seen, the small-capacity classes did a great deal to relaunch racing in Europe and to give it the truly international character it had lost since the war. But the results of the races showed that high performance was often accompanied by a lack of reliability in the engines. Whether it was better to develop power units specially for speedboats or to adapt car engines was a debate which went back to the beginning of speedboat history, and this was confirmed by

an article in *Le Yacht* at the beginning of 1926 as that year's important racing season opened.

"As for which engines will be used by the American competitors, it must be recognized that no marine engines specially built for the 1.5-liter class exist in the United States. Only car engines with this capacity can be used, and among them mainly those made by Miller, which have already shown their sterling qualities in motor racing. But adapting these engines for speedboat racing is still a problem, and it will present American engineers with the same difficulties as have faced their British counterparts in recent years. Until recently this challenge was contested in Great Britain by racers powered by car engines, but last year the trophy was won by an engine built and tuned for this international competition. So this year, we will see marine engines and ordinary engines pitted one against

the other, and it is probable that what we already know in favor of the former will be amply confirmed."

The magazine returned to this subject again in May 1926, in connection with the announcement of some new engines for the 1.5-liter class which were intended for the Duke of York's Trophy:

"It seems that the aim of this competition has been rather lost from view. The intention of those who promoted this trophy was to encourage engineers to build engines with a high output which were nevertheless not so expensive that they could not be sold commercially. Now, if we can agree that considerable progress has been made, we can also say that engineers and builders have little regard for cost because what they are seeking is publicity."

In fact, a new engine was just about to create a sensation, because it came from the workshops of Parry Thomas, who held the World Land Speed Record at 193mph. In his workshops at Brooklands, the finishing touches were being put to an in-line eight-cylinder engine which had a special firing order designed to protect the crankshaft from the effects of torsional vibration up to 7000rpm. At the same time, the Sunbeam company announced its new 1.5-liter four-cylinder. In just a few years, this class saw considerable power increases: the Sunbeam engine, which gave less than 65hp in the beginning went on to deliver more than 93hp, mainly because of progress made with superchargers. Most of the victories by British racers in this class can be attributed to Sunbeam.

MILLER ENGINES IN THE WATER

The three members of the North American delegation which came to England to compete in 1926 were all equipped with eight-cylinder engines of 91ci. The origin of these engines, which Harry Miller adapted from those used in motor racing, can be found in the continuous exchange of ideas between himself and Duesenberg during the first half of the 1920s. These eight-cylinder engines were small-capacity versions of larger engines, and sometimes proved fragile. They were symbolic of American attempts to take an interest in the European small-capacity class, which the U.I.Y.A. hoped to turn into a truly international class.

In fact, after the British victory in 1926, the Duke of York's Trophy went to the United States with the Miller-engined *Little Spitfire* in 1927; but this Anglo-American duel did not have a great future. The popular racers in the United States ran in the 151ci class which consisted mostly of four-cylinder boats, as the historian Griffith Borgeson explains in his book on Miller: *"A few hydroplanes in the 151 class used*

modified Duesenberg eight-cylinder engines, but four-cylinder types dominated the races, principally Ford and Star engines modified with overhead valves. This domination was due quite simply to the type of timed course with its tight turns around a buoy, for which the better low-speed torque of the four-cylinder was more effective in giving a rapid exit from the turns."*

A RETURN TO THE SPEEDWAY

In April 1927, *Miss California*, piloted by Dick Loynes, easily won the event at Palm Beach in Florida thanks to her new Miller four-cylinder engine. The most interesting races that year were in the 151 class.

As early as 1926, the young Californian champion had noted the development limits of the engines of that time. To quote Borgeson again: *"Loynes asked Miller to design an engine for him that was simple, a four-cylinder twin-cam which was not highly stressed and which could have its power increased at a later date if necessary. A few months later, Miller had come up with an eight-cylinder two-valve marine engine of 310 cubic inches, based on his Model 122 which had won so many victories. Goossen designed half of*

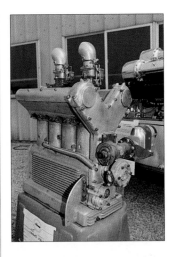

The Miller 151 Marine Racing engine was designed in 1926 for speedboat racing and went on to have enormous success in motor racing as well.

This was a four-cylinder engine with twin camshafts and two valves per cylinder. After 1930, it gave birth to the famous Miller-Offenhauser and later Offy families of engines. Engines derived from this one dominated the Indianapolis speedway for many years.

The *Angeles*, entered in the 151 class, was powered by a four-cylinder Miller engine. This is the original 1927 boat, which has now been restored.

This is a rare example of the Pelican series of 16.5 ft racers, designed by John Hacker.

the 310 engine following Loynes' recommendations. The little engine proved to be as durable as a diesel, had the acceleration and reliability which the client wanted, and made Loynes practically unbeatable in national and international competition. When the exclusive agreement with Loynes ended the following year, Miller built and sold the Marine 151 engine in quantity."

This twin-camshaft Miller four-cylinder engine started life in a boat but went on to enjoy the most extraordinary career in motor racing. It was entered in the Indianapolis 500 Miles race in 1930, opening a new era which would see several mutations of the Miller firm and its creations. Under the name of Offenhauser—"Offy" for short—the many versions of this engine derived from the original marine engine of 1926 continued to run at Indianapolis right up until the Eighties.

A DISAPPOINTING TURNOUT IN EUROPE

The few indications of activity recorded in Europe were due to the repeated initiatives of a few enthusiasts, among whom the indefatigable Dr. Etchegoin deserves special mention. The *Sadi* family of racers continued to grow, and over the summer of 1927 *Sadi VI* was launched at the at the naval boatyard in Sartouville, directed by Jouët. This new boat was registered in

the international 12-liter class, and was powered by a version of the evergreen 180hp Hispano-Suiza V8 engine. *Sadi VI* went on to better the performance of *Sadi III*, and her Picker-designed shape resembled that of the earlier boat, itself clearly inspired by *Baby Bootlegger*.

America also inspired another figure in French speedboat history. This was Marcel Jalla, who took delivery of his new racer *Yzmona III* in 1928. This was a John Hacker design, 25 ft long with a beam of 6 ft 11 in. It was a classic hydroplane with a V-section hull and no step, built of double-skinned mahogany by the Malo Lebreton boatyard at Neuilly-sur-Seine and powered by a 180hp Hispano-Suiza engine. On her first trials around the Ile de Jatte, Marcel Jalla and his faithful mechanic Rezzonicco took the boat beyond 47mph, which suggested that excellent performance would be available after tuning. But on the whole, activity in France and her neighboring countries revolved around one or two important meetings where the same boats turned up. It was the same story in the biggest 12-liter class as in the small-capacity 1.5-liter class, where attempts at international agreement failed to bear fruit after 1927 and 1928.

Meanwhile, a remarkable event took place in May 1927 which seemed to have nothing to do with speedboat racing,

but had some important indirect consequences for the development of speed on the water. Charles Lindbergh crossed the Atlantic in an aircraft powered by an air-cooled engine. This feat considerably increased confidence in this type of engine, and the new airlines went on to exploit the reliability so dramatically proven by the *Spirit of Saint Louis*. As this was a time of peace, many manufacturers slowed down their work on water-cooled engines, particularly in the small and medium capacity ranges.

Nevertheless, a few brave Englishmen from different backgrounds brought some new blood to the sport.

LAND, SEA, AND AIR
Major Hane Segrave, a great figure in motor racing, was bitten by the speedboat bug in his mid-1920s. His growing

The Wood brothers gang took the invincible armada of *Miss America* boats from victories to records.

The picture on the left was supposed to show the members of the team as other competitors saw them during a race, and on the right they are seen at a cup-giving ceremony.

Gar Wood, seen here at the wheel of *Miss America V*, always gave a welcome to challenges from the rest of the world intended to rob him of his trophies and records.

When the arrival of a new challenger was announced, it was the opportunity Wood needed to build a new Miss America, *more powerful and faster than the last. The result was always the same until this American pilot—nicknamed the "Silver Fox"—eventually retired from the sport.*

appetite for speed records led him to tilt at the twin crowns of land and water from 1928. Not long after a short period of apprenticeship at the helm of his racer *Miss Alacrity,* Segrave obtained finance for a project to build a new boat. He called her *Miss England,* a name which made clear his intention to challenge the unbeatable *Miss America* boats.

The new boat's construction was entrusted to the British Power Boat Company, directed by the talented and ambitious Hubert Scott Paine, who had spent 10 years guiding the fortunes of the Supermarine company, famous for the racing seaplanes it built for the Schneider Trophy. *Miss England* was designed by Fred Cooper, and was a stepped-hull hydroplane with a length of 26 ft and a beam of 7 ft; without her engine, she weighed less than 1100 lbs. The mechanical elements were the work of Captain J.S. Irving, chief engineer of the Humphrey Sandberg Company. Irving had been involved in the creation of the Napier-engined *Golden Arrow* record-breaker with which Segrave would tackle the World Land Speed Record.

The hull followed the latest aviation technology in being assembled with supple joints, and to save weight the pilot and mechanic sat in wicker seats. There were buoyancy tanks fore and aft, filled with ping-pong balls. The engine compartment stretched almost the full length of the keel and was occupied by a 12-cylinder Napier "Lion" engine with three Claudel carburetors and an output of 900hp at 3300rpm. There was magneto ignition; the closed-circuit

This clock is installed on the platform used by the course committee. It was the most common method of starting races at the time. *Pictures of American races always show large numbers of spectators. The Gold Cup and the Harmsworth Trophy attracted crowds of up to half a million people.*

The first racer made of Duralumin to appear was *Cigarette IV*, which was entered in the 150 mile Sweepstake at Detroit in 1926, a major event. *This prototype had to be withdrawn as the result of a fuel tank problem. Designed by F. K. Lord and built by Brewster and Company in New York, Cigarette IV was rapidly brought up to scratch and won the President's Cup soon after her first appearance.*

cooling-system was cooled by the water outside; power was taken forward via a complicated clutch system to a primary shaft which drove a gearbox, and this in turn took the drive back to the propeller shaft which turned at twice engine speed. The stainless steel rudder pivoted on the stern-post, which served as a support for the screw. In the cockpit, the wheel also controlled a second rudder well forward below the hull. This was an idea patented by Scott Paine who had obtained times of 2.5 seconds for 360-degree turns when he had tested it on some 7 ft hulls. The forward section of the keel as far back as the step was adjustable, doubtless to

After winning the Gold Cup two years running with *Baby Bootlegger*, Caleb Bragg had *Rascal* built by the Purdy boatyard in 1926 so that he could enter the Dodge Trophy.
Pictured is the modern reproduction of the boat. Like other well-known pilots, Caleb Bragg turned his back on the Gold Cup to enter competitions which had more liberal regulations. It is unfortunate that the attractive hull of the new Rascal carries large lettering which is very different from the original.

Racing boat and seaplane.
In the beginning, seaplanes had been the offspring of motor boats, but in the 1920s the press increasingly used aircraft to cover the major competitions.

allow the angle of incidence to be altered and to allow trials in different configurations.

Over the winter of 1928, *Miss England* was put on show alongside *Golden Arrow* in the London factory of Roots, the makers of superchargers. Both the boat and the car would soon leave the shores of Britain for their respective attempts to take speed records away from the Americans.

THE *MISSES* AT MIAMI

The first run-off with *Miss America VII* took place in Miami on March 20, and 21, 1929. Segrave had already been in Miami for several weeks and had broken the World Land Speed Record on Armband Beach with *Golden Arrow*. *Miss England* had hardly even been tried out when she arrived in Miami, but the new boat exceeded 87mph in a straight line the first time she was put into the water.

It was a long time since there had been such a tight contest between the Americans and the British. *Miss England* proved faster in a straight line, and *Miss America* caught up in the turns. The American boat eventually won, but not without difficulty. Her slight superiority was shown by a better timed performance of 94mph over the mile, a figure

114

A group of elegant spectators at the Baltimore speedboat races in 1927.

The course is in front of the line of large yachts, one of them carrying a full complement of flags. The woman in the hat is pointing at the scene, which seems to hold these spectators enthralled.

Horace Dodge takes the microphone to give his views of the race at Washington in September 1926.

Racing and speedboats were his whole life. Dodge was a fearless pilot and a bold constructor with great wealth at his disposal. He did not miss a chance to link his name with important events and important boats of his time. Seen here is Baby Watercar, one of his Gold Cup boats; the hull is the restored original, but the original 24-cylinder Duesenberg engine has been replaced by a 330hp Chevrolet V8.

Joy on board the *Imp*, which won the Gold Cup in 1929. This single-step hydroplane was designed and built by Purdy.
This boat had a Wright engine. She was one of those associated with the revitalization of the Gold Cup when new and more relaxed regulations authorized stepped bottoms. The hull of the Imp still exists in good condition and will probably be restored.

Sadi VI, *belonging to Dr. Etchegoin of the YMCF. Sadi VI is a boat belonging to the 12-liter class; she has a French-built hull and a French-built 180hp production engine, and she holds the world record at a speed of 65.99mph.* [It was actually 65.90mph]. *Gar Wood's boat may have reached 150km/h, but she does not belong in a recognized class and her two engines put out a total of 2280hp. Segrave's boat, which has not proved wholly satisfactory in recent trials, has a 1000hp engine. It is easy to see that the big difference in power gives only a relatively small difference in speed. The performance of Sadi VI is a great success for French industry, because no other boat in a recognized class has been able to beat the record established by Dr. Etchegoin two years ago."*

THREE LIONS FOR MISS CARSTAIRS

From *Le Yacht* magazine's point of view, the new challenge which Miss Carstairs threw out to Gar Wood for the Harmsworth Trophy in 1929 seemed far removed from any preoccupation with the relationships between weight, power and speed. This young Englishwoman's huge wealth came from her father, who was a major shareholder in Standard Oil, and she had already had some success in her first outings on the water with her 1.5-liter racer *Newg*.

Miss Carstairs decided to challenge the greatest pilots of the day, and so in 1928 she had two new and much more powerful boats built. *Estelle I* and *Estelle II* proved disappointing on several occasions and also involved her in a serious accident. But these exercises simply made this brave young woman more determined, and she had a unique aim—to regain the trophy won from the English by Gar Wood in 1921. To that end, she had *Estelle III* laid down. This boat was planned with two Napier engines but was never completed. She was replaced by *Estelle IV*. Miss Carstairs' team had made a simple calculation that if Gar Wood was unbeatable with two screws, he could be beaten with three.

To make sure that she had complete control over her operation, Marion Carstairs bought a small boatyard at East Cowes in the Isle of Wight. A great deal of money was poured into the construction of the new challenger. The bottom of the hull was made of 1.5 in. thick cedar-wood and was double-skinned; all the timber used came from the same tree; and each section was specially treated to obtain the same degree of dryness. The engines, taken from the previous *Estelle* boats, were three 1927-model Napier Lion types, each with 12 cylinders in a W-shape of three banks of four cylinders, and each one putting out 930hp at 3000rpm—a figure which suggested that 1000hp might be available at

which the American press were quick to describe as a world record. In Miami, both boats had certainly exceeded the highest speeds yet recorded, but there was a question over the homologation for the world record because their times had been established in the United States outside the jurisdiction of the U.I.Y.A. which was attempting to regulate the attribution of records.

WHAT RECORD?

It was *Le Yacht* which quickly published an interesting passage on the relationship between one set of performances and another, although these lines penned in March 1929 were rather pedantic and chauvinist.

"In view of the huge publicity which has surrounded the speed record attempts of Mr. Gar Wood with Miss America *and Major Segrave with* Miss England, *a little clarification seems in order. The only world speed record for motor boats in all approved classes belongs to France, and was won by*

3300rpm. Each engine drove a single screw geared up 3:5 through a gearbox which took the drive through 180 degrees.

The pilot's seat was immediately behind the engines. Cooling water was taken from outside the hull, which meant the boat could not be used at sea. The total weight of the boat was five tons, although the engines weighed only 1200kg: robust construction and rigidity had been preferred to a more favorable power-to-weight ratio. So this challenge seemed to be conceived very differently from Segrave's challenge, and to have been inspired by the choices to which Gar Wood had so successfully adhered for ten years. There was no technical originality to support this accumulation of brute force in the space available, and many observers wondered if *Estelle IV* had not already come to a dead end by avoiding all progress and imitating her opponent.

THE ANNUAL BALL IN DETROIT

The great annual American speedboat event took place between August 30, and September 2, 1929 in front of several hundred thousand spectators. As before, Gar Wood had refused to underestimate an opponent whose performance he had not been able to assess. He put forward *Miss America VII,*

Scotty **finished second in the 1929 Gold Cup, behind *Imp*.**

Her pilot and owner, Sam Dunsford, demonstrated both courage and sportsmanship when he turned round in the second heat to help the crew of Miss Los Angeles, which had been involved in a spectacular accident.

Scotty **is an attractive John Hacker creation which has survived the vicissitudes of time and still exists today.**

Her original Packard engine has been replaced by an Oldsmobile V8.

The hull of *Scotty* is exposed during this craning operation, and shows the multiple steps permitted under the Gold Cup rules after 1928. This alteration to the rules was intended to give new life to a class which was in decline.

So it was that almost all boats had stepped hulls after 1929. New boats like Scotty were built that way, but a lot of old racers with classical keels were reworked. This was a way of keeping costs down, because this time the crisis was primarily an American one.

officially timed at 92.82mph by the U.I.Y.A. in the unlimited class on October 1, 1928, and for good measure he also put forward a new boat, *Miss America VIII*, which closely resembled the earlier one.

Miss America VIII was 28 ft long and was powered by two 1000hp Packard V12 engines. She had the same qualities as all the previous *Miss America* boats: superior speed and a perfectly flat attitude at full speed. The suspense was short-lived, and Gar Wood retained the Harmsworth Trophy with ease. His best run was timed at an average 79.46mph, which suggests maximum speeds of between 93 and 100mph. The achievements of the hugely powerful English challenger appear modest when ranked against such performances.

Estelle IV had been finished just in time to be shipped out to the Canadian lake of Muskoka in Ontario for some shakedown trials. The English team only recognized at this stage that their heavy boat handled poorly, especially in the turns. In an attempt to improve stability, one of her Napier Lion engines had been removed, which reduced the overall weight but at the same time reduced power by

one third. So once again, it was an ill-prepared European challenger which came to measure up against a Detroit team in full possession of its powers. Before being eliminated from the Trophy by the failure of one engine, *Estelle IV* had the time to show briefly that she was not completely outclassed by her opponents. Out of courtesy, the Americans allowed the English challenger to do a second run of honor, which was actually against the rules. *Estelle IV* finished third behind the two *Miss America* boats at an average speed of 64mph.

The race was hardly over when the winning team, without its leader but with Phil Wood, set sail for Venice via Paris, where a big meeting was to be held ten days later.

A PIROUETTE ON THE LIDO

Venice welcomed the best racing pilots in the world to its first speedboat meeting, which was held between September 10, and 15 1929. The vast area of water and the complex topography of the site made communication rather difficult, but the city worked its charm on all the competitors. In the 12-liter class, the largest recognized in Europe, French and Italian boats fought it out. Count Theo Rossi's *Montalera* proved extremely rapid but gave best in the Prince of Piedmont's Cup to is compatriot *Cobar,* built by Baglietto. The French boat *Pah Sih Fou II,* with a Picker hull and a Hispano-Suiza engine, won the Grand Prix of Venice in the hands of Sigrand, while *Yzmona III,* with a Malo Lebreton hull and a Hispano-Suiza engine, was piloted by Jalla and won the Cup of the Italian Speedboat Federation. But the great international confrontation took place in the Count Volpi Cup which was open to American and English boats of the unlimited class.

The fastest boats in the world met in Venice: *Miss America V* and *Miss America VII* were ranked against *Miss England*. After a bad start in the first heat, *Miss England* confirmed the excellent impression she had made on her first outing in Miami in the spring, and took her revenge. Segrave easily beat the speed of the two American racers in worsening conditions. Before the race was over, *Miss America VII* hit a wave at full speed and leapt 30 ft into the air before crashing down again violently. Phil Wood and Orlin Johnson were slightly injured and were rescued by the crew of *Miss America V*, who went to their help. The regulations stated that when one competitor helped another, the race had to be run again. But it was all over already, and the next two heats were easily won by *Miss England* at an average of 68.03mph in the first and 70.63mph for the second. *Miss America V* had lost her starboard screw and propeller shaft in the Venetian waters.

The American press willingly acknowledged the superiority of Segrave's boat over their previously unbeatable champions, which had given their all. The *Miss America*

boats were perfectly suitable for the inland waters of the Detroit river, but things were very different in the rougher waters of Venice. The same thing had happened before when champions of the Old and the New Continents had met without success: they simply did not suit different water conditions from those they had been designed for. *Miss England* brought together a number of qualities which so often had been mutually exclusive: speed, navigability and reliability. Her performance was all the more impressive because of her lightweight construction in relation to her power, provided by a single engine. In his quest for extremes of speed, Major Segrave had opened a new way forward for Europe in 1929.

SOMETHING NEW FOR THE GOLD CUP

In the United States, two parallel class standards continued to attract the majority of those enthusiastic about large cylinder capacities. One was the Gold Cup, which imposed several restrictions, and the other was the more liberal Sweepstake. But a comparison of their respective performances reveals

the limits of the system. In 1926, the 625ci Gold Cup boats were capable of over 50mph, while their rivals in the Sweepstakes could barely exceed 60mph with twice the cylinder capacity. From year to year, the increases in the speed of these hydroplanes without stepped hulls was achieved not so much by increases in power as by a very marked reduction in their weight. The hull of *Rowdy,* a sister-ship of the *Rascal* with a length of 33 ft, was so light that her owner punched a hole in it with his fist for a bet. A single man standing at the stern could lift the hull from its cradle. These very light boats were fast but not very durable.

The Gold Cup rules, which established a minimum length for hulls, attempted to avoid extremes, but they were overturned progressively by designers and builders. To avoid killing off this great classic completely, an announcement was made in 1926 that new rules would apply for the 1928 season. Cylinder capacity would remain limited to 625ci, as before, but stepped hulls would be accepted to improve the

The Detroit Yacht Club was proud of its reputation as "the greatest yacht club in the world."
It is true that these installations seemed adequate for passing a few pleasurable hours on the water each week. Here, Gar Wood does the honors for his club with a few privileged initiates in one of his high-speed runabouts.

The assembly hall for hulls at the factory of the Dodge Boat and Plane Company in Wilmington.
In the mid-1920s, Horace Dodge threw himself into an ambitious industrial program to mass-produce runabouts. He took on the services of the highly regarded designer George Crouch.

Several firms tackled the promising market for speedboats. These are the premises of the Howard W. Lyon Corp., where V12 Liberty engines are being prepared to power luxury runabouts.

The rapid economic expansion of the United States in the 1920s ended with the 1929 crash.

speed of racers without increasing their length. Among the reasons for this decision was a study carried out by the British Admiralty. The fact was that some patrol boats with stepped hulls built for the First World War with lengths between 30 and 50 ft were capable of over 50mph, and not one of them had been lost from use in a heavy sea.

In this transitional period, the 1928 season brought nothing special in either of these classes, because the Gold Cup and the President's Cup were canceled. The first Gold Cup event which allowed stepped hulls was organized in 1929. The boats turned out to be very similar to the way they had been before the change in the rules, except that their hulls were built with one or more steps. A few older boats reappeared after being modified to suit the taste of the day. Nevertheless, the speed of the new hydroplanes was disappointing. The winner, Richard Hoyt, was timed at 50.4mph on his best run—some 6mph slower than the record for conventional hulls in 1926.

KINGS OF THE RUNABOUT

In 1927, there were 27,000,000 cars in the world, and 80% of these were in the United States. Powered boats were becoming more and more popular in the United States, although in Europe they were the prerogative of a wealthy minority—Scandinavia being an exception to this rule. The determining factor here was geography, exactly as in the case of the North American giant.

Le Yacht magazine was aware of all this, and opened its columns to various appeals in favor of the general development of powered boats, led by the example of competition: *"Sweden has 80,000 speedboat enthusiasts (without counting boats with removable engines), and America leads the dance with 500,000 boats and 300,000 with removable engines. These figures are truly impressive and give an idea of the level of motor boat activity in the New World. We wish our river authorities knew about them; they show what we should be able to achieve in France with our magnificent network of rivers."*

121

Sales of Chris-Craft boats increased dramatically after the middle of the 1920s, and the Chris-Craft name became famous all over the world.

In some countries, the name of the Algonac company became the standard word for runabouts of all types.

The beautiful finish of exterior components on Chris-Craft boats provided excellent publicity for the marque.

The chrome may have gleamed, but the runabouts of the 1920s were predominantly sober boats, with an elegance which has never been surpassed.

These statistics show the great economic importance of the market for boat and allied industries at the end of the 1920s, and demonstrate that demand within America was so great that marques which succeeded there needed nothing more to conquer the rest of the world. That is why the term Chris-Craft was for many years used to describe any kind of motorized boat. This demand is also what fired the ambitions of those who came from the motor car world and saw in the speedboat phenomenon a repetition of the irresistible rise of the automobile industry.

THE ERA OF GIANTS

Even though it had built no more than 134 Chris-Craft boats, the Chris Smith & Sons Boat Company claimed to be the world's top maker of all-mahogany runabouts after 1926. Press articles and other literature about the marque describe the Algonac factories as representing the last word as far as organization and assembly-line building were concerned, even though the 115,000 sq. ft. of covered workshops were split among 26 buildings. Another 50,000 sq. ft. were added in 1927, and further expansion followed. That year saw new

offices and a showroom well situated in the center of Manhattan, as well as the recruitment of a first-rate commercial director, and all this marked the national and international launch of Chris-Craft. The European market was put in the hands of Arthur Bray, an individual who was very influential in yachting circles and who represented England at the U.I.Y.A.

During 1928, the company had to work round the clock to meet orders, let alone build for stock. Celebrities sailed in Chris-Craft boats and outdid one another to reinforce the prestige of the company, which was exporting throughout the world. Walter P. Chrysler, who took an increasing interest in speedboats, fitted his Gold Cup racer with two in-line six-cylinder engines. The boat was a failure, but compensation came in the form of a major agreement with Chris-Craft over the supply of engines, and for many years six-cylinder Chrysler engines satisfied most of the factory's needs, which increased as time went by. Chris-Craft had no intention of allowing Dodge to forge a reputation as the only maker of popular runabouts and, despite his prestigious name, Horace Dodge did not equal the astonishing success of the Smith family.

The Chris-Craft runabout is the archetype of the American speedboat built in the inter-war period.
This is a restored example of the 26-foot model with three cockpits, which remained in the company's catalogues for many years. The influence of the earliest runabouts was still visible in the forward cockpit with its two rows of seats for four to six people.

THE REVOLUTION ACCORDING TO DODGE

In an interview for *Motor Boating* in 1927, Horace Dodge summarized the views of those industrialists who were over-reaching themselves during the astonishing American economic expansion of the 1920s: *"There is no valid reason why the manufacture of motor boats was not conceived from the beginning in a manner as effective as that of the millions of cars we now have. Even though wood is the principal material used in boats and does not allow exactly the same construction methods as are used in the mass-production of motor cars, there are certain similarities with luxury cars like the Pierce Arrow, the Packard, the Lincoln, the Cadillac and others. Twenty-five years ago, the car and the motor boat were at the same stage. No-one could have predicted that either of them would become immensely popular. Now, there are more than 20 million cars in the United States and something of the order of 800,000 motor boats). I am absolutely sure that it is possible to build boats effectively using highly standardized components which are perfectly reliable. I am convinced that this would have been possible as early as 1902. In my view, the days of building boats in scruffy sheds are numbered. If we are to mass-produce boats successfully, we*

123

need the best specialists for each phase of the work, from the purchase of the materials to the final sale to the public. We have based our range of boats on three types of hull which cover literally thousands of possible combinations. We have erected an ultra-modern factory in Detroit, which is a key position for the distribution of our Watercars throughout the country, and we are currently selling seven of them every day."

Horace Dodge was on the right track as regards the creation of his runabout models, of which the smallest was 6 ft long and carried four people. The bow of his boats was decorated with an elegant mascot, and the boats themselves were cheap and carefully aimed at the middle classes, although there were also a few more expensive models at the top of the range. A dense network of dealers was set up, which was of course essential if the products were to be sold widely throughout the country. But quality was sometimes suspect, and the sudden onset of the terrible economic crisis hit hard at those income brackets which represented Dodge's biggest potential market.

RISE AND FALL

By 1928, there were more than 20 skyscrapers in Manhattan's Grand Central District, like so many monuments

The Purdy boatyard was one of the leading places where boats were designed and built at the end of the 1920s. Its prototype hulls were in great demand because of the quality of their execution and their very light weight.

In this picture, the boatyard appears particularly spacious and clean, rather like a modern engineering workshop associated with top competition work.

The objective of the Dodge factory was to produce runabouts like cars were produced.

Horace Dodge invested considerable sums of money in effective infrastructures and in researching the processes of manufacturing wooden hulls. In spite of this, however, he came up against difficulties presented by the material itself.

124

The very name of the Dodge Watercar expressed quite clearly Horace Dodge's hope of eventually providing every American with a runabout, just as his illustrious forebears had provided them with four-wheeled transport.

The marque's expansion was aided by the full arsenal of publicity, together with credit facilities and the growing practice of marketing. At this boat show, the Dodge stand displayed a cutaway speedboat in order to counter the popular belief that a mass-produced hull could not have a robust structure. The marque took a number of promotional initiatives, because its owner had competition in his blood.

erected to an unbounded confidence in expansion. Spurred on by favorable financial conditions, the country brought its immense profits and its readily-available credit to the stock market, in the hope of instant riches. In 1928, shares attained such high levels that the point of no return seemed to get further and further away. Thousands of small investors were tempted to brave the market to have their share of the feast, and the great success which some of them had was considerably amplified by the press, so feeding the whole country's confidence in the system. Most people sincerely believed that business would always bring a just share of limitless prosperity, and that everyone was entitled to a share. It seemed almost unpatriotic to rein in the desire to buy, and frankly heretical to listen to the warnings of an economist like Roger Babson, who stated that a crash could come sooner or later. America had become a nation of consumers for whom self-persuasion had become a way of life. Then suddenly, between October and November 1929, shares lost more than 40% of their global value and 30 billion dollars were lost.

Only Monster Boats Survive the Crisis

BRITISH CHALLENGES TO AMERICAN ACE GAR WOOD FOR THE HARMSWORTH TROPHY IN THE FIRST HALF OF THE 1930S DEMONSTRATED CONSIDERABLE CREATIVITY IN THE CONCEPTION OF UNLIMITED CLASS RACERS. AT THE SAME TIME, SOME WORLD SPEED RECORDS CHANGED HANDS SEVERAL TIMES A YEAR, AND THE FRENCH AND ITALIANS FOUGHT FOR SUPREMACY IN THE REGULATED CLASSES.

Two opposing concepts dominated the period 1930-1935. Miss Britain I and Miss America X ran in different classes, but the British boat represented her country's preference for light boats with engines at the rear, while the American one typified her country's large conventional hydroplanes with four engines at the front.

Hubert Scott Paine demonstrates the aeronautical structure of *Miss Britain I* outside his company's premises.
He chose an American Scripps production engine for his first single-seat racer, preferring to devote his energy to the construction of the hull.

Scott Paine at the wheel of *Miss Britain I*. This British industrialist understood the strong links which united Britain and North America.
Scott Paine's initiative was rewarded in a second-line event, the Detroit News Trophy, which he won with an American engine in a new class. This guaranteed him widespread publicity in the world's largest market without causing any offense to the patriotism of his hosts.

A crowd around the cradle of *Newg II*, Marion Carstairs' new racer in the 5.5-liter category, powered by a Gray engine.
Miss Britain I reawakened dormant ambitions.

he shock-wave from the catastrophic American stock market crash at the end of 1929 slowly spread into Europe as well. Competition activity at the top end of the motor boat world did not seem to be directly affected by it, however, and some new sporting and technological initiatives lent new interest to the great races which might easily have suffered.

One British constructor and pilot took a very close interest in the attempts to bring European and American engine capacity classes closer together. His boat, *Miss Britain I,* astonished observers when she was launched, the more so when she easily won the Detroit News Trophy in the United States during 1930. This new event was destined to promote an American category of 335ci, mid-way between the small-capacity 151ci and 225ci classes on the one hand and the Gold Cup (which was close to the international 12-liter class) on the other.

Miss Britain I was the work of the British Power Boat Company, based near Southampton and directed by Hubert Scott Paine. Scott Paine had left the Board of Supermarine in 1923, the company whose seaplanes had won the Schneider Trophy, and he had found in motor boat racing something to suit his interest in experimentation. In the spring of 1929, during the play-off between *Miss England I* and *Miss America VII* in Miami, the small single-engined boat piloted

by Segrave had surprised the American specialists by its approach, which was diametrically opposed to that of Gar Wood's multi-engined one.

One of Scott Paine's major preoccupations was undoubtedly the conquest of the American market, and he fitted *Miss Britain I* with a 135hp six-cylinder Scripps engine made in Detroit. The concept of the new English racer was thoroughly original. It was a single-seater with a rear-mounted engine, and it perfectly summed up a new British approach: the quest for the best possible power-to-weight ratio. The idea was to perfect the design of the keel and to make a hull with an extremely low freeboard which was as strong and light as an aircraft fuselage. The British victory in 1930 meant that the trophy had to be defended in England the following year. This contest, which took place at Southampton, attracted many well-known competitors including Miss Carstairs,

Would the loudspeakers at last announce a British success against the invincible Gar Wood, king of the unlimited class?

Power boat races attracted more and more spectators in the United States, and they had to be kept informed and amused.

The fifth *Estelle*, piloted by the brave Bert Hawker, would have no more luck in the Harmsworth Trophy than her four predecessors.

Young Marion Carstairs carried Her Gracious Majesty's flag proudly into battle against Britain's former colony in October 1930. After a race in which emotions ran high, she was forced to concede victory, but not before her boat had offered serious competition to Miss America VIII and Miss America IX.

129

Gar Wood retained the Harmsworth Trophy once again in 1930, at the wheel of *Miss America IX*. Here he is seen with a famous aviator, Duke Schiller, whom he took out for a memorable test run.

June 13, 1930. *Miss England II* was traveling at over 100mph on Lake Windermere when she capsized suddenly and violently.

Henry Segrave, who had only recently been knighted, was killed instantly. The press of the time made little of the fate of the rest of his heroic team, which had just established a new world record at an average of 98.69mph.

who never missed a chance to build another new boat. She had her own small boatyard build *Newg II* to a design by Porter; the boat had few original features and was very similar to her earlier racers, the big unlimited-class boats of the Harmsworth Trophy.

ESTELLE V, THE RIVAL

Miss Carstairs spared nothing in her attempt to beat the fastest man in Detroit. Her immense resources were inherited from her father, who had made his fortune in petrol, and she used them to pay for a series of challengers called *Estelle*. It appears that Gar Wood's bold adversary did not enjoy the company of men, although she made an exception for those in her racing team, and that *Newg*, the enigmatic name of her racers, was actually an anagram of Gwen.

For the 1930 challenge, the brand-new *Estelle V*, designed by Bert Hawker and supported by *Estelle IV*, was lined up against three *Miss America* boats. This American armada was designed to put up an unbeatable defense of the trophy: *Miss America V*'s performance was obsolete, and she was present as a decoy and as a reserve in case of emergency; *Miss*

In April 1931 in Miami, *Miss America IX* broke an absolute speed record, which was homologated only by the American Power Boat Association. Her speed of 101.92mph was the average of two runs over a nautical mile.

The pace was now beginning to quicken in this long Anglo-American dispute over world supremacy.

Miss England II after being salvaged. After the tragedy on Lake Windermere, Segrave's boat was refloated. Her incredibly solid structure had stood up well to the impact of a dive into the water at 100mph.

Segrave's record attempts were taken up by Kaye Don, who set off on the dangerous pursuit of Gar Wood in 1931.

A fine drizzle greeted this victory parade for *Miss England II* in the City of London. The racer had just returned from a new exploit on Lake Garda.

America VIII was a world-class boat and stood a chance of winning, but the brand-new *Miss America IX* showed that Gar Wood never under-estimated an opponent. This latest member of the family was more powerful and probably faster than the others, and she was piloted by the team's leader, who had no intention of missing the chance of a victory. If everything went according to plan, the new boat should win comfortably; on the other hand, if something went wrong, the race would still be the best possible testing-ground for improvements which would be of value in a later rematch. Gar Wood was delighted to find that he was opposed by a boat which was potentially very fast. *Estelle V* was as new as *Miss America IX,* and the meeting looked like being an exciting one.

The great day arrived. The starter had just allowed the monstrous boats off the leash. *Estelle IV,* with Miss Carstairs on board, started well and passed ahead of the second British boat, two of the *Miss America* boats quickly nosed ahead and seized the lead. At the end of the first run, the spectators at the starting-line were amazed to see the competitors as they emerged from behind an island: *Estelle V* was preparing to do battle with the two Americans. At the wheel, the boat's designer Bert Hawker was gradually catching up the ground he had lost to his opponents at the start. He had 2600hp at his disposal, while the Wood brothers had around 2200hp. The fight became closer than ever and despite their very comfortable lead, *Miss America VIII* and *Miss America IX* began to feel the pressure from their pursuer and had to increase speed slightly.

LOSS OF A FLOATING BOMB

The Harmsworth Trophy course on the Detroit river led towards the mouth of the huge Lake Saint Clair. There was enough room on the banks for several hundred thousand spectators, but the topography of the place was such that one part of the course was out of view of the spectators, even if they had binoculars. Thanks to the presence of an aircraft with a photographer on board, it has been possible to reconstruct the main elements in an unexpected turn of events which took place on the course out of sight. *Estelle V* actually passed the two *Miss Americas* and took a defi-

nite lead in the Harmsworth Trophy, but a few seconds later two mechanical problems arose as she led the American boats. Her fuel tank split, and at the same time an oil pipe came adrift. The position of the fuel tanks behind the cockpit minimized the consequences of the leak, and although a great deal of fuel spread around the cockpit, it did not catch fire. But the hot oil escaping from

Gar Wood's performance in Miami did not go unchallenged for long.

After a brief series of trials in Europe, Kaye Don took to the waters of the River Parana in Argentina, where he broke the record set by Miss America IX with a timed average of 103.48mph over the measured distance on April 2, 1931.

A rare opportunity to get close to Miss England II.

Visitors to the London Motor Show of 1931 were able to satisfy their curiosity and admire the two Rolls-Royce R-type V12 Schneider Trophy type engines, which gave 4000hp.

Kaye Don already held motor racing records: the lap record he established at the Brooklands track in Britain in a 4-liter Sunbeam stood for a long time. He then tackled the World Land Speed Record at Daytona Beach with the *Sunbeam Silver Bullet.*

At the beginning of 1932, the Thornycroft employees were busily working on *Miss England III*, which had to be ready as quickly as possible to challenge the World Water Speed Record and the Harmsworth Trophy later that year.

Kaye Don was to be the pilot.

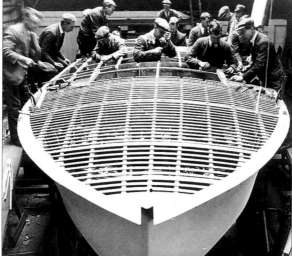

one of the engines sprayed the two men on board, and Bert Hawker's goggles were completely covered in hot black liquid, blinding him temporarily.

Estelle V was traveling at full speed, and her mechanic, also unable to see, could not get to the fuel tap. At over 85mph, the boat swerved across the bows of *Miss America VIII,* narrowly avoiding a terrible accident. The cockpit was by now awash with petrol, and this 8,000 lbs floating bomb continued on its crazy course, left the racing channel and plunged into the middle of a flotilla of boats carrying spectators. Miraculously, no-one was hurt. The crew of *Estelle V* finally managed to clean off their goggles and to regain control of the boat by reducing her speed a little. Pilot and mechanic then demonstrated an extraordinary degree of level-headedness: they reconnected the oil pipe, still traveling at speed, and without pausing the

Englishmen returned to the racing channel and took up the race again.

The two *Miss Americas* had continued on their way and were only a few hundred meters ahead when the British racer reappeared in hot pursuit. But Bert Hawker's noble fight lasted just a few minutes; the brave challenger ran out of fuel and stopped for good in mid-river. The Harmsworth Trophy rules stated that any boat which had to be towed would be disqualified, and for the second run only *Estelle IV* remained in contention. Marion Carstairs made the sporting gesture of allowing the rescued crew of *Estelle V* to take this boat, but it was already clear to the Wood team that they had won the race: for all Hawker's skill, he could not perform miracles with a boat which was clearly inferior. To retain his motivation, Gar Wood decided to break the records he had established during previous victorious runs, and *Miss America IX* ran the second leg at an average of 77.4mph, a speed never attained before.

On July 18, 1932, Kaye Don and his two mechanics beat the record held by *Miss America IX* with a speed of 119.75mph on Loch Lomond.
Gar Wood announced that he was waiting for his challenger in Detroit with the most powerful racing boat the world had ever seen.

With a power-to-weight ratio of 1.49hp per kg, *Miss England III* held a technological record. The chances of winning the *Harmsworth Trophy back from the Americans had never been so good, and Kaye Don's trip to Detroit was filled with promise.*

135

Miss America X was 38 ft long and was powered by four supercharged Packard V12 engines with a total power output of 6400hp.

On the right is Orlin Johnson, Gar Wood's faithful mechanic and the man responsible for the good running of this floating powerhouse. The Harmsworth Trophy remained in Detroit, even though Kaye Don put up a magnificent and spirited fight in front of more than half a million spectators.

TWO SEAPLANE ENGINES FOR *MISS ENGLAND*

Henry Segrave faced up to Gar Wood on the water at Miami shortly after taking the World Land Speed Record in Florida, but he had never tackled the Harmsworth Trophy with his highly original single-engined *Miss England I*. He persuaded his patron Lord Wakefield to finance a new and more ambitious project. Segrave decided against calling on Hubert Scott Paine again, whom he accused of a tendency to take all the praise for operations he took part in. So a more traditional team was formed around the naval architect Fred Cooper and the Saunders boatyard, with two aims: to take the World Water Speed Record and to win back the Harmsworth Trophy from the Americans.

The new racer was designed with scientific care, drawing on both aircraft and car technology, as the long series of wind-tunnel tests made clear. *Miss England II* was 38 ft. long and 10 ft. 10 in. wide; with her two Rolls-Royce Schneider Trophy R-type engines, each giving 1850hp, she had a power-to-weight ratio of 1.49hp per kilogram. This can be compared with the 1.58hp per kilogram of a Supermarine racing seaplane of the same year. Her screw was machined from a single block of steel and had been very carefully researched. It had a particularly small diameter of 10 in. and a pitch of 13 in., and its speed of rotation reached 12,000rpm—an extremely high figure for the time.

The choice of a single screw for propulsion may appear surprising. The engineers in the team explained the small diameter by the need to reduce its torque reaction. The idea

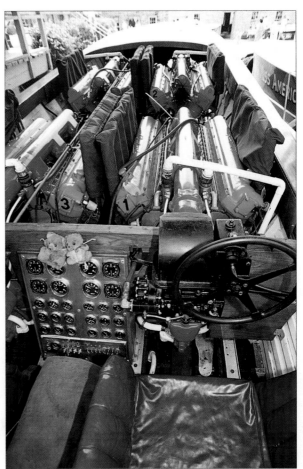

The description of *Miss America X* is a challenge to find the right superlatives, because Gar Wood never underestimated his opponents.

His response to the British challenge in 1932 was indicative of the technical and sporting reputation of the Miss England III team.

Gar Wood, the "Silver Fox", was a popular hero in the United States. His social success, his invincibility in sport, and his family life were just what the press of the day wanted.

Miss America X has survived— or at least her hull has. This is well preserved and offers new generations an irreplaceable testimony of the excess of the 1930s.

Although her engines are by Packard and the dashboard carries Gar Wood's lucky mascot of two teddy bears, none of these items is the original.

of using twin screws had been rejected because of the greater drag caused by the larger number of ancillaries trailing in the water. A lot of work had also gone into the mounting for the engine and transmission, and had led to a self-supporting structure made of interlaced beams around which the hull simply acted as an outer envelope. There was the same V-shaped step in the hull as had been seen on the first *Miss England*, with a depth of 2 1/2 in. at the sides and

In 1933, *Miss Britain III* launched the ultimate challenge of the inter-war years for the Harmsworth Trophy. After *Miss Britain III* was beaten, people began to wonder whether there was really any point in prolonging this competition.

Apart from Marion Carstairs, recent British competitors had chosen not to try to match the constant increases in power of the Miss America boats. This time, Miss Britain III attempted the impossible with the smallest and least powerful of all the challengers.

4 1/4 in. in the center. The boat steered by a system of fore and aft rudders coupled together.

SIGNED "VORTEX"

On Friday June 13, 1930, Major Segrave set out on Lake Windermere with his magnificent white boat to attempt the highest speed ever recorded on the water. Towards the end of his attempt on the measured distance, *Miss England II* see-sawed and then capsized at full speed; Segrave died shortly afterwards of his injuries. There was a sad epilogue to this tragic end, when the U.IY.A. took several weeks to ratify Segrave's world record of 158.8km/h over a nautical mile. The United States had expressed some reservations about the validity of the attempt in view of the confused circumstances in which it ended, but finally agreed to accept it. It was a unique example of a record title attributed posthumously.

The death of this gallant British pilot aroused worldwide interest, and the press reported a number of theories about the cause of the accident. One of the columnists for *Le Yacht*, who wrote his weekly column under the pseudonym of Vortex, invited opinions. The Swiss designer Picker interpreted the accident like this: *"In a boat with a single screw, there is a well-known tendency for the boat always to turn in the same direction unless something corrects it, such as the angle of the propeller shaft or the rudder. Under torque, if the screw turns clockwise, the hull tends to turn to the port side. This phenomenon can be corrected*

when the boat is fully in the water, but it can no longer be corrected when the boat is almost completely out of the water. In Segrave's accident, Miss England's screw was turning at 12,000rpm. Segrave was on his fifth or sixth run, and the water was not calm. At 95mph, the boat was almost totally on the surface and was moving forward in a series of leaps. The bow needed only to hit the water fairly hard. Several tons of force plus the torque locked up in the boat would be released, and the more the weight was transferred to the rear, the more swiftly the boat would capsize."

At the end of 1930, an American pilot knew better than anyone that Segrave's sacrifice had not been in vain. British supremacy in the world of pure speed had made it abundantly clear.

Hubert Scott Paine's racer was about five times less powerful than *Miss America X*, but she put up a good challenge against Gar Wood.

The Harmsworth Trophy remained in the United States, but the brilliant British boatbuilder left with his reputation enhanced and a full address book.

Miss Britain III **was a 7.35-meter aluminum racer with a single 1375hp Napier engine. The characteristics of her keel—a stepped hydroplane type—aroused the genuine admiration of American observers: this boat presented an original and dangerous challenge.**

Scott Paine had brought together the lessons learned from all the earlier attempts and the experience gained with Miss Britain I, of which certain characteristic features reappeared in the new boat.

MISS AMERICA X AIMS AT 100MPH

Over the winter of 1930, Gar Wood put the finishing touches to his racer. What he had in mind was a record attempt at Miami in the spring. Four superchargers were specially prepared for the two engines of *Miss America IX,* whose total power output was now 2800hp. This was the first time that a boat in the long line of *Miss Americas* had forced induction.

In Miami, the course was prepared with great care. Electric cables were stretched the full length of the water between the two fixed points, which were exactly one terrestrial mile apart, and the American Power Boat Association chose a team of official timekeepers and some sophisticated electrical equipment capable of recording the time to a thousandth of a second's accuracy.

At the beginning of April, Gar Wood put his boat into the water and did a few runs to familiarize himself with the circuit. As soon as he judged the conditions were right, the officials manned their positions. On the first test run, *Miss America IX* cleared the mythical 100mph barrier, and recorded an average of 101.14mph over the two legs of the circuit, out and back. This was the highest speed recorded in the world, but it could not be considered as a world record. The U.I.Y.A. regulations recognized only those records established over a nautical mile of 1852 meters. Gar Wood did not intend to let any legal argument get in the way of his performance, so he had the course lengthened slightly and this time achieved an average of 102.55mph. He thus beat his own record, even though the result was still not ratified by the U.I.Y.A. But would anyone have dared to challenge him?

MISS ENGLAND II SAVED FROM THE WATER

Anyone who had witnessed the terrible accident which befell *Miss England II* would have had some difficulty in believing that this boat would return to competition after she had capsized at 95mph. However, that was the wager made in 1931 by Kaye Don, who styled himself as Major Segrave's successor. The British racer's hull was known to be solidly built, thanks to a structure of large-section ribs linked by cross-braces. These cross-braces formed a large X between each set of ribs, a cross-piece reinforced by riveted aluminum. In addition, the planks were covered on their inner faces with plates of Duralumin.

A number of reconstructions have been inspired by the racers of the 1920s. It is extremely difficult to fault most of them on the grounds of taste.

This is an excellent replica of *Delphine IV*, originally built in 1925 for Horace Dodge to a design by George Crouch. She was initially named *Solar Plexus.*

The original boat has now disappeared. She had been abandoned on a beach for six years before being taken back by her owner, modified, and renamed. The Detroit pilot finally saw his dream come true: he brought the Gold Cup back to his native city.

During the first half of the 1930s, the best Gold Cup racers were "old" boats of the 1920s whose hulls had been updated by the addition of multiple steps, so that they were right up out of the water most of the time. *Delphine IV won the Gold Cup in 1932, and is seen here in low-altitude flight.*

The reconstruction of boats like *Delphine IV* presents the opportunity to bring about marvelous juxtapositions of metal and wood, like the steering sector and propeller here.

The refurbishment was entrusted to the workshops of Rolls-Royce at Derby. It appears that with the exception of the step in the keel, the boat had not been damaged much. The mystery of why *Miss England II* capsized had still not been definitively explained, and the experts continued to debate the origin of the impact which destabilized the white racer. The official English version inclined towards a collision with a piece of wood which pierced the keel ahead of the step; others still pointed to the dangerous rotational tendency of the boat around its single screw. It was the official explanation which prevailed, and only the step was rebuilt and reinforced.

Kaye Don tried the boat briefly in Ireland—where she was timed at 101mph—before having her sent to Argentina for a new attempt on the record. This very likable British driver was known for his courage; he had established the lap record at Brooklands with the old 4-liter Sunbeam. In March 1930, he made an attempt on the World Land Speed Record at Daytona Beach with another Sunbeam, the *Silver Bullet*. The *Silver Bullet* was not powered by aero engines but by a pair of V12s specially designed by the engineer Louis Coatalen. The machine was designed to exceed 250mph, but the new engines had difficulty in delivering their full power. The best Kaye Don could achieve was 198mph, which was not enough to take the record. With *Miss England II*, however, he was sure he had a craft which could win the other coveted world title for him.

A few days after Gar Wood had set his new record at Miami, the Englishman started his attempt on the Parana river, in Argentina. In April 1931, Kaye Don broke the record from *Miss America IX* with an average of 103.48 ft., a performance which improved considerably on the record set by Segrave in June 1930. This time, the new British challenge for the Harmsworth Trophy appeared extremely dangerous to the Americans. A match was set for September. On her return from Argentina, *Miss England II* was tested again before she embarked for her destination in the United States: she recorded 110.24mph on Lake Garda in July, which was enough to give Detroit's kings of the water some sleepless nights.

141

500,000 SPECTATORS GATHER ALONG THE RIVER BANKS

The announcement of the greatest match in the whole history of power boating, between the United States and the rest of the world, had an effect on the public unlike any seen before. More than 500,000 people stood waiting for hours on the banks of the great river to watch the race. The first leg was planned for September 5 but was postponed for a day because of a strong wind which whipped up a heavy swell. In the hope that conditions would be calmer at the end of the day, the start was agreed for 17.30hrs on the next day.

Shortly before 17.25, *Miss England II* was towed slowly towards the start line to the applause of a huge crowd. Kaye Don and his mechanics prepared to start their two Rolls-Royce engines. There was a fondness for dramatic effects in the American camp, so *Miss America IX* and *Miss America VIII* roared over the horizon towards the start at almost full speed. On the starter's platform, visible to everyone, yellow discs were used to indicate the number of minutes to the

"off". The last disc fell. The *Miss Americas* raced towards the line at full speed, but Kaye Don managed to get the better start and negotiated the long curve of the first turn, close up against the buoys, at almost full power. The unthinkable was happening before the eyes of the stunned crowd. After six laps at this astonishing pace, the English boat was so far ahead that she was 2km distant from her closer pursuer, *Miss America IX,* and almost double that in front of *Miss America VIII. Miss England II* finished her best lap at an average of 95mph, while the better American competitor recorded just 89.28mph. The match everyone had waited for seemed to be living up to its promise. The English victory in this first leg was an extraordinary event and one of the best sights there has ever been in the history of motor boating.

For the following day's race, well over half a million spectators crowded onto the banks of the Detroit river, starting at 9am even though the start was not scheduled until 17.30. The officials of the Detroit Yacht Club prepared them-

Delphine IV **greets her admirers with a swagger. The great majority of racers in the 1920s were varnished, but painted sides appeared at the beginning of the 1930s.**

It appears that this made their identification easier. White was generally chosen in this period, and made a happy contrast with the blue of the water.

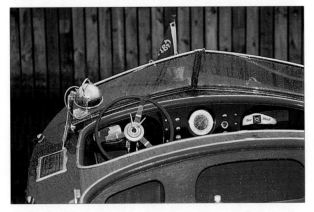

The restored *Miss Crude* was pictured during tests to tune her Hispano-Suiza V8.

This very pretty 1920s racer had her sides painted in the 1930s. She had a long career in the Gulf of Mexico in the hands of Texan oilmen.

The large runabouts of the early 1930s offered unequaled space and comfort. The great marques which had come through the 1929 crisis continued to offer their high society clients boats which were as fast and as powerful as their cars.

The lifestyle of these Americans who lived at the water's edge would have been inconceivable without their Gar Wood or other Hacker craft with three cockpits.

selves for victory by the English boat, and displayed their trophy in the clubhouse window so that it was close to the landing-stage where the race would end. The idea was that they would be able to give the trophy to Kaye Don as soon as he had finished, in order to give the news cameramen the opportunity to film this moving ceremony before darkness fell. The most enthusiastic spectators found out how much it would cost to cross the Atlantic and even booked reservations in order to be sure of seeing the return match in England next year.

At 17.25hrs, Kaye Don was ready for the "off" after a long ovation. Accustomed to the utter reliability of his superb engines, he did not start them in advance but waited for the starter's final signal. There was one minute to go before the starting-pistol was fired, and Gar Wood once again appeared on the scene in *Miss America IX* at full speed, but this time he crossed the starting-line nine seconds early. Kaye Don had taken care to synchronize watches with Gar Wood a few minutes before climbing aboard his boat, and was startled. Without thinking, he punched the starter button and tore over the line six seconds before the official time in hot pursuit of the American.

The two boats were disqualified immediately, but nothing could stop their headlong race. *Miss America IX* was 100 ft. ahead at the first turn; Kaye Don adopted his previous day's tactics and attempted to round the turn as close as possible to the buoys. While *Miss America IX* regained her line at the exit of the turn and opened her throttles fully, Kaye Don, immediately behind, had to pass through the American's wash. Seized by his desire to win, he too opened the throttles fully, but before his racer had finished sliding around the curve. *Miss England II* was unbalanced, heeled over, and turned sideways. Her prow rose towards the sky, and the boat capsized. A few seconds later, two men were swimming around her hull while a third had already climbed to safety on the bottom of the boat. The men were unhurt, and the tough *Miss England II* got away with some more major repairs.

WAS GAR WOOD DISHONORED?

The start of the second leg was certainly open to criticism, and provoked the indignation of a good number of journalists and observers of the sporting community, both internationally and in America. It seemed clear that the valiant

143

The big runabouts of the 1930s were used only as leisure boats. So to satisfy sporting clients, Chris-Craft offered a limited "competition" edition, based on the very popular 26-foot model with three cockpits.
This is Madoshumi III.

English challenger, so close to an uncontested victory, was the victim of a maneuver he was unable to resist. *Miss England II* was the only British boat, whereas Gar Wood had two boats. Many people thought that Gar Wood had deliberately started nine seconds early in order to get himself disqualified and to draw Kaye Don along behind him as a way of getting him eliminated as well. The Englishman had no experience of this kind of competition against a cunning and united team like Gar Wood's, and it is very possible that Wood realized he was unable to beat Kaye Don in the regular fashion and chose an extreme option which would allow his second boat, *Miss America VIII,* to win. Despite some long and detailed denials in the press, Gar Wood was unable to dispel all doubt and convince everybody of his good faith. His team retained the trophy in 1931, but this was no glorious victory, and from now on there was a shadow over the greatest motor boat race in the world.

Le Yacht magazine echoed a general feeling of dissatisfaction with the way the Detroit race judges had handled the affair and with Gar Wood himself. *"It has been proven once again that the English have no chance of taking the trophy back to England unless they send three boats of* Miss England's *class. Last year,* Miss Carstairs *came home utterly heartbroken, in her own words. One way or another, the judges decided not to award the trophy this year—which is, incidentally, against all the rules—while the American team satisfied all the requirements for retaining it."*

The argument rumbled on through the autumn of 1931, especially in the columns of the French weekly: *"Will we see the disappearance of the British International Trophy? The stubbornness of the Americans makes it seem likely. Not that races for large speedboats should be stopped; on the contrary, they attract increasing numbers of spectators, and at least half a million watched the last exploit in Detroit. However,* the English are the only ones to make challenges of this kind, and they are beginning to wonder whether the task they have set themselves may be an impossible one."

Gar Wood hoped he could disperse the unpleasant atmosphere created by his apparently permanent hold on the Harmsworth Trophy by tackling a new record. This time he took *Miss America IX* up to 111.66mph. There was no reply from *Miss England*, now back in her home country, and the two boats never ran together again. But by winning one leg of the race at Detroit, the English challenger had shown that she could beat the American. She was the only one to have done so and the only one not to have suffered from mechanical problems. The use of just a single screw did pose problems at very high rotational speeds, but *Miss England II* had survived two violent accidents thanks to her incredibly solid construction. After such an experience, it may be that the English team led by Kaye Don did not want to test the saying that accidents happen in threes by using the same boat. So a third *Miss England* was laid down in the boatyard.

Madoshumi V is a very rare survivor of the small run of Chris-Craft Special Raceboat Runabouts.
This boat, which won various events in 1934 and 1935, has been restored and fitted with a new Chrysler eight-cylinder engine of 450hp.

To promote the sporting activities of boats in this series, the great competitions of the 1930s had special categories. There was strong competition, but on a more friendly and sociable level.
Her racing career now over, Madoshumi V has settled down to a life of luxury in calmer waters.

No Respite for *Miss America*

In May 1932, Lord Wakefield and Kaye Don launched a third boat. She was registered in the unlimited class, and she was built with two aims: to set a world speed record which would last for a long time, and to bring back the Harmsworth Trophy to the club of its origin. *Miss England III* would also demonstrate the latest British naval construction technology for high-speed boats. This time, the hull was built by Thornycroft and Company.

An attempt was made to gather as much information as possible about the accidents which had involved *Miss England II*. The lines of the keel with its single step were finally settled after some lengthy tests with models propelled by rockets. The mahogany hull was double-skinned and had a third layer running from the bow to the step; this was the area which had given way and had let in water in Segrave's fatal accident on Lake Windermere.

The engines of *Miss England II* were the same as those of the earlier racer, Rolls-Royce R-type V12s identical to those fitted in the Schneider Trophy Supermarine seaplanes. The power of each engine had been increased to 1975hp at

The small Century boat *Thunderbolt* lives again after her restoration. It is not exclusively the preserved big boats that are interesting; the small classes for inboard-engined boats also made a major contribution to the rise of motor boat competition.

The Chris-Craft company was born out of competition. Its founder, Chris Smith, had been building the best hydroplane racers since the middle of the century's second decade, and his creations won some of the greatest races.

Fifteen years later, the small boatyard became a big company, but its sporting heritage was not lost, as is evident in this picture of Madoshumi V.

146

3000rpm, and there were twin screws which turned at 7000-8000rpm. Calculations suggested that the British boat should exceed 124mph. A lot of effort had been made to get an exceptional power-to-weight ratio. The boat was 35 ft. long and 9.5 ft. wide, had 300hp more than *Miss England II* and was 800 lbs lighter. All this gave the remarkable ratio of 3.3 lbs per horsepower, which in itself was the new boat's first world record.

Kaye Don had two mechanics on board, and his centrally placed seat was offset slightly to starboard in order to equalize the total weight of the three men about the central axis of the boat. The first serious speed trials were held on Lake Garda in Italy before the confrontation with Gar Wood in Detroit. *Miss England III* had been launched with a flourish, and this new threat from his most determined rival produced a response from Gar Wood which was in proportion to his fears. The boat was called *Miss America X,* and was the largest racer of this line ever built. Her characteristics were a list of superlatives, with an 38 ft hull enclosing four supercharged Packard V12 engines of 2495ci, each giving 1600hp. The engines were coupled in pairs and drove two screws at 7500rpm.

Over the summer of 1932, tension mounted when *Miss England III* broke the World Water Speed Record at 119.75mph on July 18, at Loch Lomond. The record she broke had been held by *Miss America IX.* Gar Wood reacted immediately by announcing that he was preparing to retake the title.

SUMMIT MEETING IN DETROIT

September 1932. The great day had arrived. Since the early hours of the morning, an immense and varied flotilla of boats crowded with spectators had been gathering along the banks of the river in Detroit. Everything that floated had taken to

the water that day, from the largest motor yacht to the frailest skiff. Every boat was so overloaded with people that several observers wondered how the authorities could allow such great danger to the populace. But the sight of the launches belonging to the coastguards and to the police—themselves totally overloaded—made clear how much law and order had been relaxed. Enthusiasm for this top-class duel was so great that it seemed as if the world had stopped turning.

The start time drew nearer. *Miss America X* was very impressive, and *Miss England III* no less so. The exhausts of the two boats produced deep earsplitting sounds which made everything vibrate for several miles around. Sailing conditions were hard because of a swell. The starting signal was given by a flashing red light, and *Miss England III* surged ahead. For three days, Kaye Don had seemed to make light of the difficulties presented by this stretch of water, while Gar Wood kept his distance and seemed to have everything under control. His prudence was well known, and he knew this stretch of water better than anyone. Suddenly, just before the end of the first leg, *Miss England III* seemed to have difficulty and slowed down enough for *Miss America X* to catch up and pass the finishing line first. Officially, the English challenger had broken a throttle control, but she was able to return under her own power and avoid a tow with its inevitable disqualification. The public accepted this first disappointment, still

Thunderbolt gets off to an excellent start at Miami in April 1931, in the race reserved for the brand-new 125 category.
The Century boatyard was the first to catalogue these small "ready-to-race" 16 ft hydroplanes. The base version had a 60hp Gray Marine Blue Streak engine.

Americans loved leisure boating on their immense stretches of water.
Runabouts offered another kind of freedom, but it was better not to abuse this: this fleet of Chris-Craft boats freshly delivered to the Chicago Police were there to keep things under control.

overcome by the fabulous sight of these two monstrous boats pitted one against the other on this vast stretch of water.

The second leg was run two days later. The story was told that the winner prepared his boat carefully with a team of 40 mechanics, while the Englishman quickly repaired his broken control, changed his engines' 24 spark plugs, and then went off to relax outside the city. After the start of the second leg, the previous year's scenario was repeated once again: *Miss England III* took the lead while *Miss America X* seemed to have serious ignition problems. In fact, both boats were pouring out black smoke and, for the leader of this crazy dance it was the beginning of the end: his engines soon gave up the ghost. Gar Wood was watching for the slightest sign of weakness from his adversary, and he once again took advantage of his challenger, now incapable of going the distance in the tough conditions at Detroit. *Miss England III* had nevertheless proved that she was a very fast boat by achieving the best time over one leg, with 88.68mph as against the American's 87.38mph. Gar Wood wanted to be absolutely certain not to attract the sort of criticism his rodeo tactics of the previous year had provoked, and so he took great care over what he did and easily retained the trophy.

THE CRITICS ARE LET LOOSE

The disappointment which the mechanical failure of *Miss England III* caused was equal to the hopes which her performance had encouraged. A section of the American press judged the preparation of the English challenger extremely harshly. No-one called into question the skill of Kaye Don, who was well liked for his decency and sportsmanship; the English champion himself admitted that he was not mechanically minded. Observers tried to find the underlying reasons for such a bitter defeat when, more than ever before, all the ingredients of a superb match had seemed to be in place, and there was criticism of the small amount of work done on the boat during the two weeks before the race. Similarly, the result did not seem to justify the atmosphere of secrecy with which the English team shrouded its activities. It was said that *Miss England III* had not even done one complete reconnaissance run around the course, but just a few test runs in front of the extremely luxurious boathouse which had been put at the team's disposition.

The Americans did not hesitate to blame the world speed record which the English racer had won just before she traveled to the United States. It does in fact appear to be true that *Miss England III* had been simply lifted out of the water onto her launching cradle after the record run, and then shipped as she was to the United States without even so much as a checkover. Journalists noted that the Rolls-Royce engines had failed more than once, although derived from those in the successful Schneider Trophy seaplanes, and were quick to attack the poor use of public funds in England, which allowed the development of engines which were very powerful but extremely

Gar Wood was a marque which benefited from the exploits of its illustrious founder.

The marque name is visible on the step of this speedster, the sporting model of the range conceived just before 1935.

The Gar Wood boatyard was the only one to offer clients a boat designed exclusively for pleasure and for speed.

As a sporting boat, the speedster made no compromises; having fun was a serious business.

expensive and had doubtful reliability. It was said that Gar Wood had to manage without support from any other body, and that he had to buy the best available production engines with his own money. Each one of his Packard engines was less powerful than the Rolls-Royce types, and having four of them on board *Miss America X* was a safety factor.

A close examination of the American racer revealed no sophisticated solutions, but only a very careful preparation of each and every detail—even the smallest. It appeared that *Miss England III* had lacked the irreplaceable element of experience. Others stressed the consequences of Segrave's premature demise. A few voices were raised in regret that the financier Lord Wakefield had not chosen to entrust the operation to the people who had made such an excellent job of the preparation of *Miss England* before Segrave's fatal accident.

SCOTT PAINE'S RETURN

Hubert Scott Paine, the former head of Supermarine,

remained faithful to his resolutely innovative choices and surprised all the specialists when he presented his new machine.

Miss Britain III grew out of the experience gained with *Miss Britain I* and *Miss England I*, piloted by Segrave. She was a single-engined two-seater, made out of aluminum; the

Wood Too is a replica of the 22 ft, 400hp Gar Wood speedster. *The well-fitted cockpit right at the stern behind an endless foredeck offers an invitation to enjoy the formidable acceleration of the Mercruiser V8 engine. There is also a small cockpit forward of the engine, seen closed in this picture. It is a remarkable experience to sit here.*

The sun will never set on this classic runabout powering across the water at full speed.

Thanks to their owners and to enthusiasts all over the world, these symbols of liberty are still with us, restored or reproduced, and are now recognized for what they are and cherished.

keel had a single and very marked step; the single rudder was at the front below the keel; and the engine was a 1375hp Napier Lion. Although this power output seemed low for a Harmsworth Trophy challenger, the power-to-weight ratio of 2.5 lbs per horsepower looked competitive.

Results quickly confirmed the excellence of the new English star. On September 23, 1933, during trials at Poole, Scott Paine and *Miss Britain III* broke the record set by the late Major Segrave, at 103.43mph. Unfortunately, a serious fire broke out on board the aluminum boat, the mechanic

was quite seriously burned, and the Napier engine was destroyed. There was very little time left to rebuild the challenger, which was due to go to Detroit to erase the terrible disappointment of *Miss England III* from the memory of the 500,000 spectators who saw her. The Americans respected the varied talents of Hubert Scott Paine, whom the press liked to describe as a "charming Englishman". The difference in size between *Miss Britain III* and *Miss America X* was remarkable, but the performance of the British boat demanded admiration. Even though Gar Wood retained his trophy once again, the press did not run out of praise for the qualities of *Miss Britain III,* which was said to represent the greatest technical accomplishment since the invention of the hydroplane. No argument tarnished the excellent performance of the two competitors. Scott Paine had a first-rate reputation in the United States, and he was able to turn this to profit by drawing up plans for the fast patrol boats of the US Navy. Unfortunately, rather less effort went into the American Gold Cup racers.

PLANING HULLS IN THE GOLD CUP
At the end of the 1920s, the rules governing the Gold Cup

A few female faces appeared from time to time at the heart of the male-dominated world of mechanized power.

Just as in the automobile and aviation spheres, many women braved the old taboos of society and took a very active part in the adventure of pioneering speed on the water. This picture shows Miss Thelma Smith, winner of the American championship in the 151 (2.5-liter) class in 1931.

Yzmona V is one of the most glorious of French racers. She broke the world record in the 12-liter category with a speed of 77.79mph on July 4, 1933.
This was the largest U.I.Y.A. class, equivalent to the Gold Cup. At the beginning of the 1930s, it was a straight fight between the French and the Italians, one reason being that the Americans were not very interested in recognizing Brussels's authority in the sport.

Emancipator III belonged to the 125 class. Boats like this in the small-capacity classes would have a profound effect on the design of racers.
The first fruits of this evolution were visible in 1934 when Emancipator III *won the President's Cup in Washington at an average speed of over 44.74mph.*

September 1934, during the Volpi Cup at the Venice Meeting.
Yzmona V *fights courageously against* Miss Britain III *in the foreground, despite a considerable power difference: 320hp for the French boat and 1375hp for the English one.* Miss Britain III *was credited with an unofficial record of 110.10mph, remarkable for a single-engined boat.*

Yzmona V was designed by Maurice Auché and built at the Chauvière boatyard at Vitry-sur-Seine in the suburbs of Paris. On the right, in the port of Cannes, Cheri Oh *is a former Sadi entered in the 12-liter class.*

A rare picture of Maurice Vasseur, the most successful French pilot of the inter-war years in the inboard-engined classes of the U.I.Y.A.
The holder of several world records and winner of several cups, he was sponsored by wealthy sportsmen who clubbed together to finance a new racer for him every year.

had been made more flexible, and hulls with multiple steps had been allowed. one effect of the 1929 slump had been to put the brakes on competitors' spending. For that reason a number of older racers reappeared; built in the 1920s, they were rebuilt to suit the taste of the times.

So it was that the 1930 event was won by *Hotsy-Totsy*, a boat built in 1926 whose hull had been modified after the fashion of *Rainbow IV*, 1924's disqualified winner. *Hotsy-Totsy*'s striking name came from a fashionable song of the day, and she won again in 1931. The 1932 race was won by yet another veteran with a modified hull. *Delphine IV*'s had multiple small steps, and the boat seemed to have been transformed into something akin to a seaplane float; at full speed, she seemed to spend more time in the air than on the

A view of the *parc fermé* at the Meeting de France held in Paris during 1934 alongside the *Alexander III* bridge.

Policemen in cloaks are keeping a close eye on the racers belonging to the Italian competitors, who were the most threatening adversaries of the French.

Lia III belonged to the 12-liter category and was piloted by Count Becchi. She had a Baglietto hull and an Isotta-Fraschini engine. She was beaten to the world speed record in 1933 by the French boat *Yzmona V.* Lia III *is pictured here at Herblay on the occasion of the Paris Meeting. The bright sunlight does not appear to trouble the Italian crew in their impeccable white overalls. The Duke of Spoleto, standing, has come to support his fellow-countrymen.*

water. Next it was the turn of an old acquaintance to win the Gold Cup: *Miss Mary* had been built to a Hacker design in 1922 and was renamed *El Lagarto*. She won the 1933 event easily, and repeated the feat in 1934 and 1935 as well.

This triple victory by a boat more than ten years old is indicative of the most important changes in the event over more than a decade. The changes in the rules were like some sort of elixir of youth, as multiple-step hulls gave significant performance improvements without demanding any increases in power. But the struggle for supremacy was still between competitors from the Detroit region and those from the East Coast. In 1933, the Gold Cup left Detroit for Lake George, a summer resort favored by wealthy New Yorkers.

Further changes in the rules did prove necessary, however, even though the most serious consequences of the crisis had been avoided. From 1935, supercharged engines were permitted in order to maintain interest in the event, and before long all the restrictions on hulls would also be removed, thus opening new fields for experimentation and keeping the event's credibility intact.

A REAWAKENING IN EUROPE

While the Gold Cup was finding its way in the United States, there was a revival of interest in European events, especially in the most powerful class. Competitors did not hesitate to cross the borders of their own countries to take part in the major events held in France, Italy, and even Germany, where the Potsdam International Meeting was revived.

It was at this meeting in June 1930 that the French put forward *Pah-Sih-Fou IV* and *Pah-Sih-Fou II*, which won a splendid victory over the Italian racer *Montalera* piloted by Count Rossi. In the cruiser class, several Chris-Craft boats took part in events organized by the marque's European importer, Arthur Bray, where there were several prizes to be won. The next meeting was in Paris on July 12 where two events were held: the Sixth Seine Motor Boat Meeting of 1930 and the European Grand Prix for Speedboats. The races were beginning to grow in size and the boats in the 12-liter class made a magnificent spectacle. *Montalera, Sadi III, Sadi VII* and *Pah-Sih-Fou IV* put up a fierce struggle for victory.

A strange incident during the first heat made clear how fierce the competition was: with the pressure on, *Sadi III* turned at the wrong buoy on the downstream run, only to be followed by *Montalera* in hot pursuit. That first heat was won by *Sadi VII* with an average of over 54mph. But the spectators were to see more of this stirring stuff when the Italian racer *Montalera* caught fire during the third and final heat. Count Rossi was obliged to jump overboard while his burning boat careered off towards the yachts moored on the bank. But the fire aboard *Montalera* was quickly extinguished, and her Celli hull and Isotta-Fraschini motor were repaired in time for the Venice Meeting a few weeks later. The Grand Prix was meanwhile won by *Pah-Sih-Fou IV*.

Performances improved year by year. In June 1931, Dr. Etchegoin won the French Meeting at Herblay with his *Sadi III*, powered by a Hispano-Suiza 12-liter engine. His best run was at 62.51mph. The duel between the French and the Italians dominated the first half of the 1930s, and this time the French *Sadi III* was opposed by the Italian *Venezia*, a Celli-hulled boat which averaged 59.9mph on her best run. A new name also appeared in the lists, that of *Incognito IV*. This was not a new racer but the former *Pah-Sih-Fou II*, which had embarked on a new career. The victory of *Sadi III* in this Grand Prix was the occasion for the magazine *Le Yacht* to pay tribute to Dr. Etchegoin, whose passion for speedboats had led him to build a new one almost every year: *"He is always the same refined sportsman, always able to enjoy himself as much as he thrills the spectators. He tackles even the most mundane races with the skill and care which have always led him to victory in competition."*

The sporting calendar was enriched by a new event when the first Geneva Meeting was held on August 15, and 16 1931. Shortly afterwards, the competitors met up again in Venice for the traditional event on the Lido at the end of the summer. Maurice Vasseur was slightly injured during a record attempt with *Sadi III*, which was fortunately refloated shortly after the accident. *Yzmona III* won the Mussolini Cup, piloted by Marcel Jalla.

THE RECORD YEARS

Prince Maurizio Ruspoli broke the world record for the 6-liter class in his boat *Niniette II*, with a speed of 63.29mph on November 12 1931. The earlier record had been established in the United States by Hubert Scott Paine with *Miss Britain I*. *Le Yacht* magazine reported that the design of *Niniette* had been inspired by the lines of the late Major

Asso had a hull by Baglietto and an Isotta-Fraschini engine, and belonged to the 12-liter class. She illustrates how the French and the Italians swapped records and victories in the 1930s. The engine in this Italian boat was one six-cylinder bank of the V12 Schneider Trophy engine, known as the Asso. *Asso took the world record from Yzmona on August 15, 1933, at 83.17mph. That year, Italy held the official records in all the U.I.Y.A. classes for boats with inboard engines—the 1.5-liter, 3-liter, 6-liter and 12-liter classes.*

Dr. Eugenio Etchegoin at the controls of *Sadi*, which had a Hispano-Suiza V8 engine. Note the details of the construction and planking, visible in this picture.

With the exception of Sadi III, *all the Sadi boats took their inspiration from American racers designed by George Crouch. That was a fair trade, since so many American championship boats had been powered by engines of French origin.*

Segrave's *Miss England I*. The boat was built by Celli in Venice, and had a 4.9-liter eight-cylinder Bugatti engine which delivered 260hp.

Three days later, Italian sportsman Count Becchi took his boat Lia III out onto Lake Garda to beat the world record in the 12-liter category with a speed of 69.09mph. This was a blow for the Dr. Etchegoin, holder of the previous record of 67.68mph with *Sadi VI*. Becchi's racer was a pretty Baglietto hull with an Isotta-Fraschini engine. But the new record was not immediately homologated by the U.I.Y.A. because the paperwork was not complete. Then at its annual meeting in Brussels, held from 26–28, November, the U.I.Y.A. broke new ground in the globalization of its activities by admitting Australia. In its final report, there is an interesting definition of the runabout category. A runabout is defined as a boat without a stepped hull which can carry at least five adults in comfort. The report also states that a runabout is not a racing boat, and cannot therefore be used to break records.

THE FRENCH AND ITALIANS TAKE IT IN TURNS

Although there was an increase in the number of meetings being held, the best French and Italian pilots were mainly concerned with record attempts. New records were established regularly on both sides of the Alps.

Racers were modified so that their performance would keep on getting better. Thus in May 1932, *Sadi VIII* did her first test runs at Herblay—although her hull was in fact that of *Sadi VI*, with its bottom reinforced with Duralumin in order to withstand high speeds, and the step moved 4 in. further aft. The boat caught fire during a practice session for a record attempt, and her indefatigable pilot Dr. Etchegoin had to jump overboard, fortunately unhurt. Luckily, the fire was quickly brought under control and the boat was not badly damaged. But this incident marked the decline of the great *Sadi* line, and a glorious new era for French racers was about to open. On June 29, 1933, *Yzmona V* took a world speed record over the terrestrial mile, at 77.78mph.

In the 12-liter class, the previous record of 69.09mph had belonged to Signor Becchi and *Lia III*. The record was broken at Vitry-sur-Seine in front of the Chauvière boatyard, which had built the record-breaker. *Yzmona V* weighed some 2500 lbs, and was a single-seat racer with a double-stepped hull designed by Maurice Auché. Her engine was a 320hp Hispano-Suiza V8 which ran at 2800rpm, with gearing giving a speed of 3800rpm at the propeller. Like the other

A big crowd at the *Alexander III* bridge watches *Incognito XI* pass at full speed during the French Meeting in July 1932. This 12-liter boat was the former *Pah-Sih-Fou II*.

157

boats in the *Yzmona* series, *Yzmona V* belonged to Marcel Jalla and Maurice Vasseur, who was also her pilot.

THE ITALIAN APOGEE

The annual Venice meeting was held from August 11, to 15 1933, and was dominated by excellent performances from *Yzmona V,* which won a magnificent victory in the Cup presented by Amédée de Savoy, Duke of Aosta. This splendid meeting on the Lido attracted the best European boats, and witnessed the traditional record attempts on the terrestrial mile. A new racer attracted the attention of all the observers present: this was the *Asso,* built by the Baglietto boatyard for the 12-liter class and powered by an Isotta-Fraschini engine. On August 15 *Asso* took back the record so recently broken by *Yzmona V.* She was piloted by Guido Cattaneo, and achieved an officially recorded speed of 83.15mph.

The year 1933 was a particularly good one for Italian competitors. Mussolini could be proud of his highly enviable position as leader of a country which held the world speed

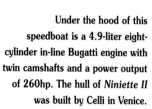

The most highly developed of a series of boats to bear this exotic name, *Pah-Sih-Fou IV* belonged to the 12-liter class.

The boats all belonged to Monsieur Sigrand, the owner of a successful clothing chain. Pah-Sih-Fou IV was powered by a Hispano-Suiza V8 engine.

Under the hood of this speedboat is a 4.9-liter eight-cylinder in-line Bugatti engine with twin camshafts and a power output of 260hp. The hull of *Niniette II* was built by Celli in Venice.

Prince Maurizio Ruspoli won the world record for the 6-liter class with this boat on November 12, 1931 at a speed of 63.3mph. In this picture, the pilot is Divo, who won the President of the Republic's Prize at Paris in 1933.

In 1931, *Venezia* was one of the rare European boats within an officially recognized class to have her engine in the stern. *Venezia* belonged to the 12-liter class.

Her hull was built by her pilot, Celli, and she had a Hispano-Suiza V8 engine.

records in all the official classes of 1.5 liters, 3 liters, 6 liters and 12 liters. This domination continued into 1934.

A LAST RECORD FOR *YZMONA V*

It was once again at the Venice Meeting that the most interesting European confrontations were to be seen. In September 1934, there was a remarkable match between two boats with very different power outputs. For the first time, *Yzmona V* met *Miss Britain III* in the Volpi Cup. The English racer had covered herself in glory during 1933 in a desperate race against the super-powerful *Miss America X,* which had some five times as much power. This time, it was the turn of the English boat to be some five times as powerful as her French adversary. Maurice Vasseur put up a tremendous

fight at the controls of the French boat, while Hubert Scott Paine was the pilot of his own aluminum single-engined boat. As was to be expected, *Miss Britain III* was the winner, although *Yzmona V* was by no means totally crushed. The champion Vasseur had no intention of leaving Venice without a new title, and in a final attempt on Sunday October 21, 1934, he broke the record for 24 nautical miles in the 12-liter class with a speed of 77.81mph.

In the various European classes, stepped-hull hydroplanes—usually with their engines mounted forward—ended the first half of the decade with a veritable harvest of records. But the period which was just about to open would witness their final decline, for a revolution which had started in America was afoot.

Three Points . . . of Suspension

THERE WAS A RESPITE IN THE ANGLO-AMERICAN DUEL FOR THE WORLD RECORD. IN THE LARGE-CAPACITY CLASSES, GOVERNMENT AID TO THE AERO INDUSTRY PROVIDED THE EUROPEANS WITH EXCELLENT ENGINES. AS FOR THE AMERICANS, WHO DEPENDED ON CAR ENGINES FOR THE SMALL-CAPACITY CLASSES, MOST PROGRESS WAS MADE IN DESIGN. A NEW TYPE OF HULL KEEP DEVELOPED IN THE UNITED STATES MADE AN IMPACT ON COMPETITION ALL OVER THE WORLD.

Aurora was the first and only unlimited-class French hydroplane, and was launched in 1935. This type of stepped hull was about to die out in favor of a new structure, known as the three-point type, which would remain unbeatable up to the eve of the Second World War and beyond.

The River Seine below the bridges of Paris was host to a festival on Saturday July 6, 1935. In the very heart of the capital, the Spreckels Trophy event was being held for the first time. This international challenge cup had as its prize 150,000 Francs put up by Madame Jean Dupuy, *née* Spreckels, in memory of her brother. She was the wife of the great French outboard champion and, as the daughter of an American sugar baron, her considerable fortune enabled her to sponsor a number of initiatives in the speedboat world.

Up-river, the course was defined by the Louis-Philippe bridge, while its other end was about a mile downstream at the Carousel bridge. Turns were to be made around the piers of each bridge. It was a delightful course, but the important originality of this event lay in the fact that it was open to all types of small-capacity engines. So the list

of entrants brought together some very fast outboard-engined boats, like that of the eventual winner Jean Dupuy, and some small inboard-engined racers such as *Uncle Sam,* piloted by Stanley Dollar and fitted with a supercharged 91ci Miller four-cylinder engine and an outboard transmission. This was an interesting event and was much liked by the Parisians, but its hybrid character limited its scope, and it was clear that changes in the rules would be necessary.

The Internationale de Yachting Automobile meanwhile held its annual convention in October 1935. Its business was to continue trying to achieve a worldwide agreement on rules. Or, to put it another way, the aim was to minimize the effects of American independence proclaimed many years ago by the American Power Boat Association.

Giving up the idea of classification by cylinder capacity and replacing it by one of weight did not exclude older boats: racers registered in the old cylinder-capacity classes before September 30, 1935 would be allowed to run in the new

Aurora is pictured during trials on the Seine in 1936. This boat was the most powerful single-engined French racer ever built with forward mounted engine.

She was later renamed Rafale V. In the position normally reserved for a racing number, she carries the symbol of infinity and the number F1. The general lines of Aurora/Rafale V represent a style typical of French racers in the 1930s in the bigger classes. Her topsides seem more ahead of the times than her hull, which still had multiple steps.

Aurora was very isolated in Europe in the unlimited class, and underwent a number of modifications so that she could perform different tasks. Here she is, renamed *Rafale V,* passing at full speed in front of the Grand Palais in Paris.

In this configuration, she carries additional fuel tanks, visible as semi-cylindrical objects alongside the hood. The tanks were added so that she could attempt long-distance records.

classes but would be ranked separately. The new simplified classes established were:

1	under 350kg
2	350kg to 750kg
3	750kg to 1200kg
4	over 1200kg.

But a French initiative would deliberately go beyond these limits set by the rules.

Aurora, the First Unlimited-Class French Racer

In France, the Tecalemit company was a major supplier of equipment for cars and aircraft. It was directed by Émile Picquerez, a great yachting enthusiast who ignored the barriers which normally separated sailing from motor boating. He had a large collection of both sailing and motor boats, among them some racing yachts of international class (6 meters and 8 meters JI), as well as several large runabouts with two and three cockpits. Come winter or summer, his boats were to be seen at the Côte d'Azur or on the Seine.

Magnificently restored, *Rafale V* is seen here in her final and most spectacular form. The raised hood reveals the 2136ci Hispano-Suiza aero engine, which had a nominal output of 650hp.

163

This businessman was behind a number of highly individual racers which allowed France to retain a presence in the great international classes right up until the outbreak of war.

Picquerez was the man who ordered the greatest single-engined racer built in France in the "unrestricted" class. Boats of this class were the only ones capable of breaking the world water speed record, and until this point, only the English and the Americans had really taken up the challenge. *Aurora* caused a sensation when she was first seen in public in July 1935. Her elegant and powerful lines had been created by the engineer Galvin, a specialist in fast-boat hulls, whose name had been associated with the development of hydrogliders for transport. Many people had put their hopes into this form of communication during the 1920s, when it had been judged essential for river traffic in the French Empire, and particularly in Africa.

Aurora's wooden hull was 28 ft long, and was built by the Chauvière boatyard at Vitry-sur-Seine. Her chosen engine was a V12 Hispano-Suiza aero engine of 2196ci,

Berryla II is one of the aluminum racers constructed and piloted by the British industrialist Percy Pritchard of the Birmal company. *The original hull and its tuned 120hp Lea-Francis four-cylinder engine have been preserved, and Berryla II can still be seen on the water today.*

Parisian children watch Berryla II during the Spreckels Trophy on July 6, 1935. The course was run in the heart of Paris, from the Louis-Philippe bridge to the Carrousel bridge.

Incognito XII belonged to the French speedboat pilot Meyer. She had a hull built by Celli in Venice and a Hispano-Suiza V8 engine. In October 1937, she broke three long-distance world records at Sartrouville, near Paris.

It is interesting to note how the owners of some of the best racing boats gave appearance a much lower priority than speed and reliability. The boat is seen here in the Lyons-Marseilles-Cannes race.

modified to give very much more power than standard and supposedly around 850hp. Her hull was a hydroplane type with two steps, the rudder at the stern and a center-board. She was very solidly constructed, apparently without concern for the power-to-weight ratio, at least as compared to a single-engined boat like *Miss Britain III*. So it looks as if endurance rather than pure speed was the aim of this unique French initiative.

It is difficult to evaluate *Aurora*'s performance and potential, not least because she was completely isolated in her class in continental Europe. Later renamed *Rafale V,* she was fast and won races where she was mainly up against racers with 12-liter engines or weights of 1200kg. In summer 1936, for example, at the Cannes Motorboat Week, she won the President of the Republic's Prize with an average of 90.34km/h over the 12km course. She was piloted by her owner, ahead of *Yzmona V* with Vasseur at the controls. That same week, *Yzmona V* won the French-Italian Grand Prix ahead of *Incognito XII*, piloted by Meyer.

RECOGNITION FOR *INCOGNITO XII*

Throughout the 1930s, French racers were present in almost every class which could give rise to an international record

The team which took three world records with *Incognito XII* consists of, left to right, Vasseur, Meyer, and the great aviator Doret.

Aviators and great motor racing or motorcycling champions frequently took the controls of a speedboat during the 1930s. Among them were Sommer, Nuvolari, Varzi, Stuck, and Monneret, without mentioning the British record-holders whose interest was in pure speed.

165

In September 1938, *Alagi*, piloted by Count Theo Rossi Di Montalera, became the first European boat to win the Gold Cup.

She was the fastest, most robust and best-prepared boat of a largely lackluster group. The American opponents of the great Italian champion were simply not up to the standard of the Old Continent's representatives in the 12-liter class.

The second half of the 1930s saw some important developments in the structure of racing boat hulls.

Alagi was the last boat with a classic hull design to win a major event like the Gold Cup. Here she is, at the bottom of the picture, racing against Don Arena's Miss Golden Gate. The American boat had a new type of hull which would lead on to the "three-point" hull; note how the wake of each boat is distinctively different.

homologated by the U.I.Y.A. Thus in October 1937, *Incognito XII* won world records in the 1200kg class for three, six and nine hours between Montesson and Sartrouville to the west of Paris. She was an individual boat with her engine in the stern like the racer *Venezia* which had been seen in Paris in 1934. Like the *Venezia,* she had an Italian hull by Celli, built in Venice and equipped with a 280hp Hispano-Suiza V8 engine. The team put together for these absolute records consisted of Meyer, her owner, Vasseur, the most successful French champion, and Marcel Doret the great aviator. Mechanical problems prevented them from taking the 12-hour record at the same time.

In July 1938, *Incognito XII* won the very demanding Lyons-Marseilles-Cannes race, which covered both inland waterways and the open sea. *Aurora* also took part in this race as the only entrant in the unlimited class. The course and the sailing conditions mercilessly eliminated several boats, especially on the River Rhône, where a number of wrecks and floating pieces of wood tested the competitors' vigilance. Time spent in locks and in the Rove tunnel was of course not counted. *Le Yacht* magazine dated July 23rd, 1938 commented: *"A relatively large number of boats withdrew, as can be seen from the number of finishers, and most of these resulted not from fouled propellers but from engine failures. The 200 miles of the Rhône are a test-bed that engines are not accustomed to. A number of boats also ran aground thanks to the inattention of their pilots, who took no notice of the advice of professional pilots or of indications on the map but took bends as tightly as they could, knowing all the while that they were passing across gravel banks."*

RECORDS BY WEIGHT

At the end of 1936, the U.I.Y.A. made a few small adjustments to the definitions of its weight classes. As the Gold Cup was no longer the great contest it has been, and in order to encourage international comparisons, six boats specially built in the United States for the old 12-liter (732ci)category were officially allowed to compete in 1200kg races in Europe—regardless of their actual weight. Regular efforts were still being made to reconcile classes and records. The United States wanted records set during a race over a distance of five miles to be homologated. The U.I.Y.A. doubted that it was technically possible to establish performance figures for certain in every race. So agreement was finally reached on a Five-Mile world championship, limited to three international events: the Spreckels Trophy,

the Harmsworth Trophy, and the Gold Cup.

The United States still seemed to dominate motorboating in the world, while France and Italy clearly dominated competition in Europe. The so-called international classes established by Brussels were their private hunting-ground. The Americans were less well-equipped with engines originating from the aero industry, and still declined to join in.

THE GOLD CUP LOSES ITS SHINE ·

After 1936, in conformity with the agreements reached at the Brussels meetings, the rules of the Gold Cup category were modified again to make them more open. All engines of between 610 and 732ci were now accepted, so that European boats could also take part. At the same time, American boats were encouraged to cross the Atlantic to measure up to their equivalents in France, in Italy, or in Britain. So the Gold Cup was now open to foreign competitors, on condition that they had the courtesy to enter through an American yacht club.

It was high time for some changes to this venerable event, which had begun to suffer a worrying decline in the standard, quality and quantity of entries. At the 1936 event, only six boats turned up on Lake George, in the mountains of north-western New York State. In fact, only two of the six proved capable of starting, and only one of them managed to pass the finishing line. This made the final placings easy

The French racer *Piva* appeared in 1937 and carried the hopes of Maurice Vasseur in the 1200kg class.

The boat belonged to Émile Picquerez, who owned a stable of both sailing boats and motor boats which included Aurora/Rafale V. Like her larger sister, Piva was a Chauvière hull, with a classic stepped keel designed by Galvin. Her principal original feature was the use of a rare Farnan V12 aero engine. On July 8, 1937, she broke the world record for her class with a speed of 87.38mph.

to establish, but it hardly made for an exciting race. The winner was *Impshi,* built in 1925 to a George Crouch design and fitted on this occasion with a supercharged six-cylinder Packard engine—much more reliable than the Miller V16 with which this pretty racer was expected to start a new career year after year. It was a hollow victory for the British champion Kaye Don, who had piloted *Miss England II* and *Miss England III* to such good effect against Gar Wood and his *Miss America* boats.

EUROPEANS TRY TO CONQUER THE WEST

Not many foreign competitors entered American races, and the Americans returned the compliment. A small number of boats, mostly British or Italian, did cross the Atlantic, but sailing conditions and class differences often made the resulting matches disappointing. The very different conception of racing boats on the two sides of the Atlantic also made for some poor matches. But the year 1937 marked the beginning of a new era, because it was the first time that two Italian boats and one French one lined up for the start of the Gold Cup in Detroit.

Count Rossi had brought the two Italian boats: *Alagi,*

Impshi, a 1925 George Crouch design, is one of those racers which have aged well.

After being known as Hornet, Ethel Ruth III, and *Delphine VI, she regained her original name and was rejuvenated with a Miller V16 engine, among other things. In the hands of the British champion Kaye Don she won the 1936 Gold Cup while fitted with a six-cylinder Packard engine. She was the only boat not to withdraw.*

Painted Lady is a 19-foot Chris-Craft Racing Runabout from 1936. This small series of boats were destined for sporting clients who hoped to take part in the very enjoyable competitions organized on the margins of the great national events.

The boat shown here is the one which broke its class record in 1937 at over 50.96mph. Today, her engine is a recent 280hp V8.

which he piloted himself, and *Aradam,* which he entrusted to Guido Cattaneo, who had prepared the two racers. Both boats had been built in metal by the Baglietto boatyard, and both had six-cylinder seaplane engines by Isotta-Fraschini, of the type made famous by the Balbo Squadron's propaganda tour on behalf of Mussolini. Their names were those of two mountains in Ethiopia, a patriotic gesture which reflected the importance the Italians attached to the conquest of this old African kingdom by the Black Shirts.

France's tricolour was carried by *Rafale VI.* This was a boat from the Picquerez stable currently named *Piva* which had been renamed for the occasion, perhaps so that the American press would not confuse her with the Italian entries. She was a stepped hydroplane, with lines drawn up by the engineer Galvin, and was generally similar to his other creations. The most original feature of *Piva* was her Farman V12, the prototype of an aero engine which never did see production.

The boat had been built in wood by the Chauvière yard, and it was Maurice Vasseur who took the controls for this American adventure. The French boat proved very fast and finished in an encouraging third place in the first heat, but a problem with the rudder during the second heat prevented her from finishing the event.

The eventual winner, after three heats, was the American racer *Notre-Dame,* which featured a rear-mounted Duesenberg engine and was piloted by the same Clell Perry who had distinguished himself with his powerful Chris-Craft runabout *Madoshumi. Alagi* finished second.

The French team's tour finished in Detroit, but the Italians continued their voyage and went on to Washington to take part in the traditional President's Cup. This end-of-season race was always an important event because of the high number of participants, and in 1937 there were in fact 245 boats of all classes entered, among which were more than 110 inboard-engined types.

Notre-Dame won again, once again more because of her regularity and reliability than because of her speed. Speed was more the domain of the Italian racers, which astonished American observers. In the final placings, *Alagi* finished second ahead of *Aradam; Juno,* with a new type of hull, came fourth, even though she had capsized and was placed in only one heat. Her accident was spectacular but not serious, and occurred during a turn when *Juno* was in the lead; she took the turn at full speed because of a jammed throttle. Nevertheless, Count Rossi had good reason to be pleased with his expedition, because *Alagi* proved to be the fastest boat in the event. She posted not only the best average

speed in a heat, with 66.12mph, but also the best lap time with 91.36mph—enough to smash the US record for single-engined boats. The great Italian champion promised to return in 1938.

THE THREE-POINT REVOLUTION

The economic consequences of the 1929 financial crisis had some long-term consequences on the development of top-class racers in the United States during the 1930s. Among those which gained honors in major events (except for the Harmsworth Trophy), there were several boats built before 1927. At that time, the construction of new boats for the Gold Cup and the Sweepstakes continued at a frantic pace. It was also in this period that wealthy individuals approached Harry Miller and the Duesenberg brothers with orders for fabulous but troublesome engines with 16 or 24 cylinders which only became successful ten years later. In the large-capacity classes, American pilots created new wine from old bottles for many years, while many European racers in the 1930s used aero engines whose enormous design costs had been covered by government budgets. In the considerably less expensive small-capacity classes, engine development depended on the car, and the Americans came to the fore in this sector.

This picture, taken at the end of February 1937, shows the traditional annual regatta at Palm Beach. This festival included sailing and motor boats, and was a source of great pleasure to the people who took refuge in Florida for the winter. *Maud Rutherford is here seen at the controls of a Class E runabout, the Chris-Craft Imp II. The young Rutherford in the rear cockpit is keeping on eye on the boats pursuing his mother's.*

Jay Dee II won the free-for-all race at the Palm Beach regatta in 1935. This kind of race was open to all comers, and was generally run at the end of a long series of other events.

This Chris-Craft 26-foot Special Raceboat has been restored and fitted with a 450hp engine. It is a very rare type of runabout, capable of reaching speeds of around 50mph.

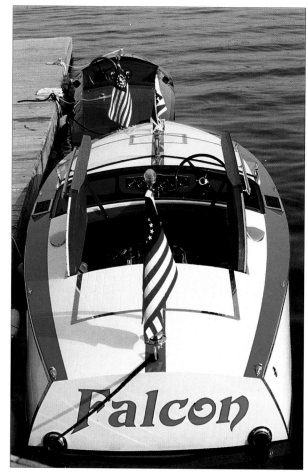

The 19-foot Chris-Craft competition boats of the late 1930s allowed many enthusiasts their first taste of battle in Class E.

The racy lines of this type of runabout represent an elegant synthesis between sport and regular usage.

So it was no surprise that the most important progress was made in the area of hull design, especially those intended for small-capacity engines where the build costs were within reach of the small boatyards and their usual clientele. It was here that the theory of three-point keels was directly applied at the beginning of the 1930s. The theory was not all new, however; its origins date back to the very beginnings of work on hydroplanes and skimmers in the nineteenth century and at the beginning of the twentieth century.

One of the most important ideas behind the concept of the three-point keel was that the smallest possible surface of the hull should be brought into contact with undisturbed water. Classic hydroplanes, with or without a stepped hull, have a large surface in contact with the water and therefore skim across water which has been disturbed, whose lift is theoretically less. One of the great advantages of a three-point keel is that each surface is carried on water which has not yet made contact with the boat and is less turbulent as a result.

This idea was already an old one by the time Adolph Apel started applying it in 1914. In the second decade of the century, George Crouch was also experimenting with such concepts for his Gold Cup racers *Peter Pan VII* and *Peter Pan VIII*. But for a period of nearly 20 years, this research lost impetus and no traces have been found of any major work done on this kind of hull.

From the beginning of the 1930s, Adolph Apel experimented successfully with evolutionary keels on a number of racing boats. Then, in October 1937 and with the assistance of his son Arno, he took out a patent covering hulls with three support points, two in front and one at the rear. In practice, the two forward points were most commonly floats, while the third was at the extreme rear, near the screw.

A Gain in Every Respect

The first small-capacity, high-performance *Emancipator* racers represented the beginning of a radical change in the conception of hulls. Next came *Miss Manteo*, the first of a long and successful line in the American 225 category. The Apel family perfected the hulls which would completely overturn world competition at its Ventnor boatyard in Atlantic City.

Starting from what was already known, the Apels made a number of decisive advances which justified their claim of invention and created an indisputable lead in the field of high-performance hulls. To the two floats and the concave hull surface behind them, they added tunnel-like shapes which trapped the air between the two pontoons and directed it towards the concave shape of the bottom as far as the

The Century boatyard catalogue offered a range of small racers known as Thunderbolts, fitted with 175hp Gray Marine Racing Fireball six-cylinder engines.

Chickie IV is a 16 ft runabout launched in 1939, and has been restored along with her original engine.

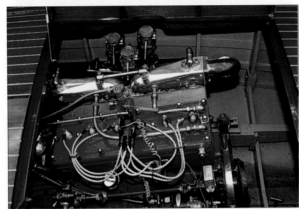

Restored racing engines today present an immaculate picture in their varnished wooden jewel-cases.

Rallies of classic boats reward collectors for the enormous care they lavish on their craft.

stern, thus improving the way the hull skimmed across the water. In this respect it is worth remembering the work done by Alfred Hickman during the second decade of the century, when he became the first man to apply the concept of two parallel hulls joined by a flat surface. His famous sea-sleds showed some remarkable qualities of seaworthiness and speed in a number of different applications.

The Apel designs made an immediate improvement to performance, and results went on to ensure an extraordinary success for the Ventnor boatyard. After *Miss Manteo* had arrived in the competition world, the speed of racers in the 225 class went up by more the 30% in two years. At every level of competition, the introduction of three-point keels became almost unstoppable. Small boats with three-point keels like *La Cucaracha* or Mortimer Auerbach's *Emancipator IV* in the 225ci class proved capable of beating the best of the Gold Cup boats with engines three times as big.

Bombs For the Japanese Emperor

From the middle of the 1930s, major cracks began to appear in the edifice of world peace as tension began to increase.

171

Chris-Craft introduced a small series of 16 ft boats with characteristic rounded stern to their range of competition runabouts.
These so-called "barrelbacks" appeared at the end of the 1930s. Dynamite is a good restored example with a 121hp six-cylinder engine.

France under the Popular Front in 1936 witnessed two scarcely reassuring facets of the European continent in the shape of the Olympic Games in Berlin and the Spanish Civil War. At the same time, the Pacific bore witness to a terrible Japanese assault on China.

The remarkable performance of the three-point racers gave ideas to those who were arming the conflict, and the Chinese Government ordered eleven boats from the Ventnor boatyard. It had become apparent that the combination of weight, power and speed displayed by the winners of so many events could make for excellent torpedo-boats. In fact,

these boats could carry 500 lbs of explosive, and a suicide pilot could steer one very precisely at 60mph into the side of a Japanese warship without risk of being intercepted. The whole exercise was relatively cheap. Out of the initial order for eleven units, only ten were in fact shipped to their destination, and fate ordained that the remaining boat should be sold to an American champion who needed a new boat for the racing season. Thus was born the extremely fast *Juno*, a boat rescued from a massacre in the sea off China which went on to have a brilliant career.

AMERICANS IN EUROPE AND AN ITALIAN IN AMERICA

The new Ventnor type hulls found their way systematically and very quickly into European competitions. The Italian pilot Castiglioni took *Argo IV* to victory in the Aero Cup at the French Meeting in Herblay in July 1937. Some good motor boat events were also held in England and Italy; American competitors came over and were well rewarded for their trouble. At Torquay in Great Britain, the Duke of York's Trophy reawakened the interest it had lost since the pilots from across the Atlantic had disappeared. The winner was the three-point racer *Emancipator VII*, a Ventnor hull powered by a Gray Marine engine and piloted by the very experienced Mortimer Auerbach from Atlantic City. In summer

May Be **is a very pretty boat designed by John Hacker and built in 1936.**
Her 150hp Gray Marine six-cylinder engine gave her good performance in her class and has now also been restored.

1938, John Rutherford took *Juno* to a clear victory in the 12-liter category ahead of *Alagi*, once again piloted by Theo Rossi. The winner claimed that Rossi was the only European capable of offering him serious competition. Rossi and Rutherford then left for Detroit, where the Italian's participation in the Gold Cup was eagerly expected.

The 1938 event was the occasion of the first and only European victory. An anecdote gives some idea of the confusion surrounding the event, when a radio commentator referred to the victory of "Count Alagi and his boat, *Rossi*." The entry list was relatively modest and a number of mechanical problems left just two competitors in the frame,

but none of that should detract from the victory of Rossi and *Alagi*, which finally showed its mettle. The winning boat was technically unchanged since it had finished second the previous year. *Alagi* was a classic hydroplane, and her victory was obtained over a single and very promising adversary from California, *Miss Golden Gate*.

THE GALLANT DAN ARENA

Miss Golden Gate was a three-point hull put forward by two talented young men. Dan Arena was just 21 years old and was the boat's pilot, designer and builder. His team-mate Dan Foster was 23 years old. They put their boat together

Franklin D. Roosevelt receives the President's Cup in the Oval Room at the White House.

This cup is traditionally given by the President of the United States to the winner of a respected race which is run every September on the Potomac River. The importance of this competition increased at the end of the 1930s as the Gold Cup lost its credibility.

173

cheaply and calmly towed her from Oakland, near San Francisco, all the way to Detroit.

These two impoverished young men made a striking contrast to the rich competitors who usually took part in the Gold Cup. To finance the trip, they had sold one of their two cars. The boat's engine was an old Hispano-Wright V8 to which a supercharger had been added. The public took a great interest in this adventure, and so did the race judges, who decided to express their admiration by awarding them a special prize.

The favorite for this event was a new version of *Notre-Dame*, which did not run because Clell Perry suffered a serious accident during testing. *Excuse Me,* a strange machine with its engine at the rear designed by the Briton Fred Cooper and put forward by Horace Dodge, literally disintegrated during the race and *Miss Canada III* withdrew after repeated mechanical problems. A new three-point Ventnor boat named *My Sin* and powered by a Miller V16 made it to Detroit but failed to start through lack of preparation. Even the most chauvinistic of observers agreed that the European competitor came properly prepared for the event, which had

A magnificent set of timing gears on one of the two impressive W24 Duesenberg engines built specially for Horace Dodge in 1926.

This engine did not prove successful until ten years later, after Harry Miller had rebuilt it to power Notre-Dame to first place in the Gold Cup.

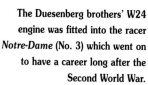

The Duesenberg brothers' W24 engine was fitted into the racer Notre-Dame (No. 3) which went on to have a career long after the Second World War.

This classic stepped-hull hydroplane was the work of Dan Arena. It was built quite late—in 1939—after its owner Herbert Mendelson persuaded Arena not to risk its magnificent engine in a "three-point" hull.

(Bottom): *Miss Canada II* passes
the White House on the Potomac
River during her victory in the 1939
President's Cup. She was designed
by Douglas van Patten and built in
Canada by Greavette in 1938.
*(Top): The modern reproduction of this
unusual racer allows us to see how her
hull behaved at high speed.*

Maud Rutherford was the wife of a
famous speedboat pilot of the
1930s. She gave a new lease of life
to *Miss Columbia*, originally built
in 1924 for the Gold Cup. Modified
and renamed *Miss Palm Beach*, the
boat won numerous victories.

The historian Griffith Borgeson
stands in front of the restored
Duesenberg W24 engine,
rebuilt by Miller.
*Borgeson has done some excellent work
on Harry Miller and on the Miller
engine family, and has established the
relationship between his car engines
and his boat engines.*

not been the case with most of her potential rivals. As usual,
the Gold Cup weekend included several races in the smaller classes, such as the 225, and these races proved the absolute superiority of the three-point hulls which rapidly
accounted for all the placings.

THE *NOTRE-DAME* RIDDLE

After 1935, the name of *Notre-Dame* turned up regularly in
records of events, but the press of the day gave few indications to help establish which boat they were writing about
each time. A comparison of results and photos makes quite

Flowing lines are characteristic of the boats built by the Canadian Greavette boatyard.

Little Miss Maple Leaf is a reproduction of Canadian champion Harold Wilson's Little Miss Canada IV. The original boat began her career in 1934 and won many victories in the 225 class during the 1930s.

The design of *Little Miss Canada IV* was by John Hacker, and its eclecticism can be appreciated in these pictures. An attractive mascot is fitted to the bow, and the sides are painted in the fashion of all the other *Miss Canada* boats.

The modern boat has a marinized Ford V8 engine, just like the original. In this case, it puts out 60hp.

clear that there was more than one boat of this name, and it is astonishing that the wealthy owner of this family did not see fit to differentiate his boats one from the other by a number—because there were four of them!

All these boats were built around the same Duesenberg engine with its 24 cylinders arranged in a W pattern, an engine specially commissioned in 1926 by Horace Dodge to power one of his *Delphine* boats. The order comprised two engines and a large number of spare parts. The experiment was not conclusive, however, and Dodge sold one of his engines to Herbert Mendelson, a major shareholder in General Motors. Mendelson in turn had a boat built for the Gold Cup, a hydroplane with front-mounted engine which became *Notre-Dame* No. 1. Designed and piloted by Clell Perry, this boat won the President's Cup in 1935. Perry modified the boat considerably for the 1937 Gold Cup, moving its engine to the rear to create *Notre-Dame* No. 2, with which he won the Gold Cup that year.

Mendelson was encouraged, and commissioned Perry to come up with a new hull for the 1938 season. This one became *Notre-Dame* No. 3, and was a rear-engined hydroplane, very broad and very flat, and resolutely original in shape. During trials for the 1938 Gold Cup she showed a promise of great speed in her constructor's hands, but suffered a serious accident. So her owner turned to the young Don Arena, who ran an extremely good race with *Miss Golden Gate*. *Notre-Dame* No. 3 was taken on by Dan Arena, who managed to finish second in the President's Cup, but the boat had a number of major stability problems which proved impossible to correct.

Dan Arena suggested that Mendelson should build a new boat, with a three-point hull. However, Mendelson's recent experiences with special hulls had probably made him wary, and he asked Dan Arena to design and build a conventional stepped hydroplane to take the Duesenberg W24. This was *Notre-Dame* No. 4, which won the President's

Cup in 1939 and after 1940 set out on a long and glorious career which stretched way beyond the end of the Second World War.

Shortly before that war began, another racer also made a very promising début.

FIRST VICTORY IN THE GOLD CUP

My Sin was the first boat with a three-point hull to win the Gold Cup, which she did in September 1939 at Detroit. It was a new victory for a boat from the east coast. *My Sin* belonged to Zalmon G. Simmons, a well-known bedding manufacturer who also took her controls. The boat was very similar to *Juno* and was built by Ventnor around a Miller V16. She was tested at the 1938 event, when the mechanical elements failed to live up to the great car designer's reputation. Shortly before the race started in 1939, Simmons declared: *"We have not modified anything on the hull, but the engine has been completely rebuilt. We have some brand-new cylinder blocks made by Offenhauser which give a total of 725 cubic inches. We have new camshafts, new pistons and new valves; and the ignition has been overhauled. The only parts of the original 1927 Miller engine are the bottom end of the engine, the crankshaft and the conrods. The boat exceeded 105mph on test, and we have increased the power by about 150hp. So we are very confident. But we think the greatest progress we have made is in the area of reliability."*

Like many Miller Marine engines, the V16 in *My Sin* could be run with or without a supercharger. For the Gold Cup, it was fitted with eight Winfield carburetors and developed around 650hp. Right up to the last moment before the closure of the entry list, there were hopes that Count Rossi would arrive; he was due in New York on August 31, with his quick and very reliable boat, *Alagi*. The tensions in

It's A Wonder is a good example of the new style which rose to popularity in the late 1930s. *The so-called three-point hulls were so effective that they gave excellent results even when powered by very old engines.*

177

The engine of *It's A Wonder* is none other than a 220hp Hispano-Suiza V8. *This restored version is less sober in appearance than those which came straight from the factory at Bois-Colombes.*

Europe justified the participation of the Italian champion, who was very much liked by the Americans. *My Sin* won in very difficult sailing conditions, beating *Miss Canada III* and *Notre-Dame* No. 3 with her rear-mounted engine. At 66.5mph, she also broke the previous Gold Cup record set by Rossi with *Alagi*.

The Europeans consoled themselves with a series of spectacular record attempts.

CURIOSITIES, EXPERIMENTS, AND RECORDS IN EUROPE

At Suresnes on November 27, 1937, *Niniette VI*, with a hull and engine both by Bugatti, beat Theo Rossi's 6-liter class record with 83.17mph. Her pilot was Maurice Vasseur. The boat was quite unique and had a new type of transmission inspired by outboard drives. The 4.7-liter, in-line eight-cylinder engine developed around 400hp at 5200rpm, and drove two contra-rotating screws. This was the only known example of a boat completely

built by Bugatti; other racers powered by Bugatti engines had been built by independent naval boatyards. The fashion for transmissions of this type started in France with inboard-engined boats.

In June 1938, Émile Picquerez carried out the first trials of his new 1200kg-class racer in the harbor at Suresnes. His aim was to take the world record from Theo Rossi, who had set it at 90.94mph on August 4 1937. This rear-engined boat had been designed by Galvin, and her right-angled transmission by Bonnemaison; in the engine room was an 850hp Hispano-Suiza V12. However, this interesting confection would not be seen again before the end of the war.

Speedboat racing and military needs seemed to be associated once again in a British initiative which was full of promise for the Royal Navy. *Le Yacht* magazine in August 1938 reflected the trials of the mysterious machine known as *Empire Day:* "*The atmosphere of mystery which surrounded the existence of Colonel Lawrence (T. E.*

The famous stork is proudly painted on the sides of the restored *It's A Wonder.*

Three-point American racers were seen in Europe, in this case at Torquay for the Duke of York's Trophy in 1938.

The arrival of a new generation of boats like Emancipator VII sparked a revival of competition. Emboldened by their success at home, many American competitors crossed the Atlantic for what amounted to a demonstration tour.

Juno shows off the shape of her keel. The age of the classic hydroplane was over.
Beginning in 1936, the Ventnor boatyard produced this new type of hull based on an Apel patent. It would go on to have applications outside speedboat competition.

Juno exceeded 88.25mph at Miami in March 1938, in the hands of John Rutherford and Mortimer Auerbach.
Her 732ci six-cylinder Packard engine performed excellently, and preparations were made to challenge the Europeans in their top category.

Shaw), the uncrowned king of Arabia, has not dissipated with his death. Even his death several years ago after a road accident has been put in doubt by those who saw in it a final maneuver by the Intelligence Service. Then time did its work, and Lawrence's name became a legend. The most recent information published by newspapers is not calculated to destroy that. The suggestion is that before his death, Lawrence had collaborated with a modest Bradford engineer on plans for a motor torpedo boat capable of reaching a considerable speed.

"The idea is not new, and several navies are known to possess torpedo boats whose great speed and small size make them relatively invulnerable. The Japanese have gone even further by putting into service the human torpedo, a machine directed straight onto its target by a suicide pilot. Lawrence's motor boat does not demand such self-sacrifice from its pilot. It allows him to get within a few dozen meters of the enemy warship, to launch its torpedo with perfect accuracy, and to have a chance of escaping defensive fire. Known as Empire

Day, *in accordance with Lawrence's wishes, it bears witness to that sense of Empire understood by every Englishman of class. Let us remember that at the height of the illness which killed him, His Majesty King George V could still find enough strength to ask, 'How goes the Empire?' Lawrence's* Empire Day *has just been tested on Lake Windermere. It showed such excellent seagoing qualities that the Admiralty is said to have ordered the construction of several examples of the type."*

The boat piloted by Edward Spurr could be fitted with two different engines despite its small size, a very modest 150hp 31ci or an imposing 960hp Napier 'Lion'. Tests were interrupted by a serious fire, from which Spurr escaped thanks to a prompt response by the rescue team. The project seems to have been abandoned, as there is no record of any boat of this type being put into service.

However, the idea of another British subject did go on to have a more glorious future.

A BLUE BIRD OVER LAKE MAGGIORE

After 1933, Gar Wood had laid up *Miss America X* and had treated himself to a comfortable retirement in Florida. Four years later, the world speed record still belonged to him, at 124.86mph. Lord Wakefield, the owner of *Miss England II* and *Miss England III,* had also retired from this extremely costly quest, and the two most valiant British racers in history found shelter at the back of a boathouse. All the pretenders to the world title had deserted the cause. The British pilots Kaye Don and Scott Paine were heavily occupied elsewhere, and no American was prepared to risk such an expensive adventure.

When a new challenge came, it came once again from the world of motor car record-breaking, and it came once again from Britain. The hero this time was one of the world's most popular sporting personalities: Malcolm Campbell bravely decided to give his career a new start on the water.

The name of Malcolm Campbell first appeared among those of the World Land Speed Record holders on September 25, 1934, when his Sunbeam reached a speed of 146.15mph on the beach at Pendine in Wales. He would take the record again eight times before September 1937, when he conceded victory to his fellow-countryman George Eyston.

This boat has an astonishing story to tell. She was originally commissioned from the Ventnor boatyard in 1936 by the Chinese armed forces, during the Sino-Japanese War.

In that war, three-point racers were turned into suicide torpedo boats and used against Japanese warships. They carried a 500 lbs bomb and were sent on their way at over 60mph. Just one hull remained in store to escape its tragic mission.

181

The last record established by the famous *Bluebird* was established at Bonneville; the car reached 301.12mph with its Rolls-Royce "R" V12 engine, which developed 2350hp at 3250rpm. It was a specially prepared and uprated version of the Schneider Trophy seaplane engine, rated for no more than 30 minutes' use. Campbell would succeed in taking the two supreme world records simultaneously, one on land and one on the water. *Bluebird I* was an 28 ft boat, designed by Fred Cooper. She was built by Saunders Roe at Cowes, with mixed construction consisting of a double skin of mahogany over a steel frame. The engine was identical to the one used in the record-breaking car, a 2150hp V12 Rolls-Royce "R"-type.

Campbell not only beat the existing record which Gar Wood had set up on Lake Saint Clair in September 1932 with the four-engined Miss America X but he also smashed the unofficial record set by *Miss Britain III*, Scott Paine's single-engined Napier-powered boat timed at 110.10mph in Venice during 1934.

Campbell was a newcomer to speedboat competition, and his record attempt almost went dramatically wrong on

Gray Goose III is seen here from an unusual angle, passing at full speed in a rising swell. By the end of the decade, three-point hulls of the Ventnor type were the subject of a variety of technical experiments.
This boat was unusual in having three Lycoming 225 engines which gave a total of 525hp. Each engine powered a separate screw.

Gray Goose belonged to the 225 (3.7-liter) class. She was a small-capacity Ventnor boat of the type which became very successful after 1937.
During tests at Miami, the intrepid Maud Rutherford reached a speed of 73.54mph to set a new record for this American class.

182

The hull of *Shadow II* was built in 1936 by the Minett-Shields boatyard in Canada.

Her current Hispano-Suiza V8 is not the original engine; as built, she had a less powerful Lycoming six-cylinder.

Victory in the 1939 Gold Cup for the superb Miller V16 built in 1926. *Zalmon G. Simmons is seen here (left) at the controls of My Sin, a three-point Ventnor hull. The Miller V16 engine is one of three built for Horace Dodge between 1926 and 1928, and was restored with the intention of using it in a replica racer. It was seen in Europe for the first time (below) at the Paris Boat Show in 1992.*

September 1, when two cooling water pipes burst and caused a brutal change in the balance of the boat. Campbell was able to draw on his experience of high speeds in cars and kept control of *Bluebird I*. On September 2, 1937, he reached a speed of 129.52mph on Lake Maggiore at Locarno—but this was not enough to satisfy him.

A New Record for Campbell

The new racer, Bluebird II, was built by Vosper Ltd. at Portsmouth. Her three-point hull was decisively innovative

Strange shapes began to emerge from the boathouses at the end of the 1930s.
Empire Day was born out of enthusiasm for records and rumors of war. T. E. Shaw, better known as Lawrence of Arabia, designed it together with the engineer Edward Spurr, seen here at the controls. The days of the British Empire were already numbered by this time, however.

In 1938, Emile Picquerez had a racer built for the 1200kg class with an 850hp Hispano-Suiza V12.
She had a unique outboard transmission with two contra-rotating screws. This boat, Rafale XI, was built to beat Theo Rossi's class record. The war caused the project to be abandoned.

as compared to *Bluebird I*, and was the joint work of Arno Apel, the patent-holder and inventor, and Peter Du Cane. Both of them were then working for Vosper. Several models were tested in a tank before the definitive choice was made. The bottom of the hull was concave and, instead of a step, there was a stabilizer on each side to increase the width. Each stabilizer was hollow and open at its rear end. A center-board was fixed to the inner section. When the boat was traveling at full speed, the forward part of the hull made no contact with the water. The hull was supported by the rear ends of the two stabilizers and the contact surface was much smaller than on a classic stepped-hull hydroplane. The boat was 27.5 ft long, whereas the older *Bluebird* had been just 23.5 ft long.

The hull was made of wood, reinforced in various places by Duralumin plates, and the engine was an R2 version of the Rolls-Royce V12 R-type, with a cylinder capacity of 2230ci and a power output of 2350rpm at 3000rpm. The screw was geared up by a factor of three to turn at 9000rpm, and starting was by means of compressed air. The total weight of around 5000 lbs was almost identical to that of the first *Bluebird*.

184

In 1937, the Bugatti workshops built *Niniette VI*, a record-breaker equipped with Bugatti's own 4.7-liter eight-cylinder car engine which put out around 400hp at 5200rpm. The right-angled transmission drove two contra-rotating screws.

Maurice Vasseur broke Theo Rossi's record in the 6-liter class with a speed of 83.15mph.

Bluebird I ended the American domination of speed records.

Malcolm Campbell made his measured runs on Lake Maggiore, at Locarno, on September 1 and 2, 1937. He achieved 129.52mph.

Surrounded by tropical vegetation, a group of Italians lend their strength to Malcolm Campbell's team as *Bluebird II* is put into the water.

The name of Malcolm Campbell was associated with the World Land Speed Record after 1924, when he reached 146.15mph at the wheel of a Sunbeam on Pendine Sands.
His final Land Speed Record was 301.12mph, achieved with the Campbell Special on September 3, 1935 at Bonneville.

On August 31, 1939, *Bluebird II* reached a speed of 141.76mph on Lake Coniston in Britain. This was Malcolm Campbell's last attempt on a world record, and was witnessed by his son, Donald. The exceptional performance of *Bluebird II* demonstrated the superiority of a three-point hull over the stepped-hull hydroplane, and the British champion's record was not beaten until 1950.

During the summer of 1939, the Union of International Motorboating let it be known that its annual meeting had been canceled because of the gathering clouds of war. The meeting had been scheduled to take place in Brussels on November 6 7, and 8th.

In addition, the news broke that the American Elco boatyard had just signed a first contract for 23 motor torpedo boats designed by Hubert Scott Paine, the designer of *Miss England I* and *Miss Britain III*. The engines in these boats were to be supercharged 2500ci Packard V12s, similar to those used by Gar Wood in *Miss America X*. Their hulls had been directly inspired by the experience of

British and American pilots in more than ten years of top-class speedboat competition. In Europe, and then in the United States, competition ceased. Offshore races of a new type, with no limitations on engine capacity, speed or fuel consumption, would fill the calendar for the next few years on all the world's seas.

After 1939, a new class of ultra-rapid boats came to dominate the international scene. The performance of the best examples owed a lot to two decades of competition.
This is the prototype of a series of torpedo-boats built by Elco, and is seen on trials. The design was by the Englishman Hubert Scott Paine, who had demonstrated his many talents to the Americans at the controls of his Miss Britain boats.

PRINTED SOURCES

– CAMPBELL, William T. Jr., *A Speedboat Scrapbook, 1920-1950*, à compte d'auteur, Downington (Pennsylvanie), 1992.
– International Sporting Club, *Exposition et concours de canots auto-mobiles*, Paris, I.S.C., catalogues, 1904-1913.
– France : *le Yacht, Yachting Gazette, l'Auto*
– Grande Bretagne : *Yachting World & Power Craft, The Motor Boat & Yachting*
– États-Unis : *Motor Boating, The Motor Boat, The Rudder, The Detroit News, The New York Times, Yachting*

BIBLIOGRAPHY

– BARRETT, J. Lee, *Speedboat Kings*, Detroit, Arnold Powers, 1939.
– BODEMER Alfred et LAUGIER Robert, *les Moteurs à pistons aéronautiques français, 1900-1960*, tome 1 et 2, Paris, Larivière, coll. « Docavia », 1987.
– BORGESON, Griffith, *Miller, Cars and Biography*, Osceola (Wisconsin), Motorbooks International, 1993.
– BORGESON, Griffith, *The Classic Twin Cam Engine*, Londres, Dalton & Watson Ltd, 1981.
– CHARLES, Daniel, *Yachts et Yachtmen, les chasseurs de futurs*, Rennes, Emom–Ouest-France, 1991.
– DESMOND, Kevin, *Power Boat*, Londres, Conway Maritime Press, 1988.
– DICKEY, Philip S. III, *The Liberty Engine 1918-1942*, Washington, Smithsonian Institution Press–National Air and Space Museum, 1968.
– FOREST, Fernand, *Bateaux automobiles*, Paris, Dunod et Pinat, 1906.
– FOSTLE, D.W., *Speedboat*, Mystic (Connecticut), Mystic Seaport Museum Stores, 1988.
– GONON, Bernard, *les Moteurs d'avion et l'évolution de l'arme aérienne : 1914-1940*, sous la direction de l'Institut d'histoire des conflits contemporains et du Service historique de l'armée de l'air, *in* Actes du colloque « Adaptation de l'arme aérienne aux conflits contemporains et processus d'indépendance des armées de l'air des origines à la fin de la Seconde Guerre mondiale », Paris, École militaire, Fondation pour les études de défense nationale, 1984.
– GUÉTAT Gérald, LEDRU Éric, *les Racers de l'age d'or, États-Unis, 1918-1929*. Paris, Yachting Heritage, catalogue de l'exposition du Salon nautique, 1992.
– HOUGH, Richard, *Book of the Racing Campbells*, Londres, Stanley Paul and Co., 1960.
– JAMES, Derek N., *Schneider Trophy Aircraft 1913-1931*, Londres, Putnam, 1981.
– LEDRU Éric, GUÉTAT Gérald, *Yachting et progrès technologiques à Monaco 1904-1914*, Monaco, Yacht Club de Monaco, 1994.
– MEAD, Cary Hoge, *Wings Over the World*. Wauwatosa (Wisconsin), The Swannet Press, 1971.
– RAMPAL, G.Clerc, FOREST, Fernand, *le Yachting*, Paris, Pierre Laffitte et Cie, 1912.
– RODENGEN, Jeffrey L., *The Legend of Chris-Craft*, Fort Lauderdale (Florida), The Write Stuff Syndicate, 1988.

PHOTOGRAPHIC CREDITS

Black & White Archival Photography
The page number is followed by the indication:
position of the photograph in the page (h for top, b for bottom, g for left, d for right, m for middle) and year when the picture was taken, for color photographs only.
Rosenfeld Collection, Mystic Seaport Museum, Inc. : pp. 9, 15 (h), 22 (h), 24, 25, 28 (h), 32, 34, 35, 36–37, 38–39, 40, 41, 42, 43, 45, 50, 51, 53, 56, 61, 62 (h), 63, 65 (d), 67 (b), 70 (b), 73 (hg), 73 (bg), 75 (h), 77 (b), 80 (d), 84 (h), 85 (h), 85 (b), 87 (h), 94 (d), 96–97, 98–99, 100, 107 (hd), 107 (hg), 112 (hd), 112 (hg), 113, 114 (b), 115 (h), 115 (bg), 117 (h), 118 (h), 120, 121, 123 (h), 124, 125, 128 (bg), 136, 139 (bg), 139 (bd), 141 (g), 143 (hd), 147 (hd), 173, 175 (bg), 175 (bd), 180 (b), 182, 183 (bg), 187 (b). **Keystone** : pp. 46 (h), 49 (b), 58, 59, 104 (b), 107 (bd), 108, 110 (b), 111, 112 (b), 119, 126–127, 128 (h), 128 (bd), 129, 130–131 (b), 132, 133, 134 (b), 135 (h), 137 (hg), 138 (b), 139 (hd), 140 (94), 144, 147 (bg), 151 (b), 154, 158 (h), 159, 165, 166, 167, 168 (h), 169, 179. **Collection Yachting Heritage** : pp. 84 (b), 93, 101 (h), 110 (h), 116, 130 (hg), 131 (h), 134 (h), 135 (b), 137 (bg), 138 (h), 150 (b), 151 (h), 153, 155, 156, 160–161, 162, 163 (h), 164 (b), 174 (b), 184 (h), 184 (b), 185 (h), 185 (b), 186 (h), 186 (b), 187 (h). **Collection privée** : pp. 28 (b), 29, 67 (b), 68 (g), 69, 70 (h), 71 (h), 78, 80 (g), 83 (h), 83 (d), 106 (h), 152 (mg), 152 (b), 158 (b). **Roger Viollet** : pp. 11 (b.), 12, 13,15 (b.), 16, 101 (b), 152 (h), 152 (md), 157. **Musée de l'Air** : pp. 21, 30, 31 (h), 33, 102. **Collection Jean Houët** : pp. 103, 104 (h), 105. **Collection Alec Giaimo** : p. 174 (h).

Color Photography
Griffith Borgeson : p. 175 (d) (93). **Gérald Guétat** : pp. 14 (94), 17 (94), 18 (94), 19 (94), 20–21 (91), 22 (b) (91), 23 (91), 27 (92), 31 (b) (94), 44 (92), 46 (b) (94), 47 (94), 48 (94), 49 (h) (94), 52 (94), 54 (94), 55 (94), 57 (94), 60 (92), 62 (b) (94), 64–65 (92), 68 (d) (91), 70 (g) (91), 71 (b) (92), 72 (94), 73 (hd) (92), 74 (94), 75 (b), 76 (h) (92), 76 (b) (94), 77 (h) (94), 80 (h) (94), 81 (92), 82 (92), 83 (bd) (92), 86 (94), 87 (b) (94), 88–89 (94), 90 (94), 92 (94), 94 (g) (92), 95 (94), 99 (b) (91), 106 (b) (92), 109 (g) (92), 109 (d) (94), 114 (h) (94), 115 (bd) (92), 117 (hm) (94) 117 (b) (94), 122 (h) (91), 122 (g) (94), 123 (b) (92), 127 (b) (94), 137 (hd) (94), 137 (bd) (94), 140 (94), 141 (d) (92), 142 (94), 143 (hg) (94), 143 (bg) (94), 143 (bd) (91), 145 (94), 146 (h) (91), 148 (g) (92), 148 (b) (92), 149 (94), 150 (h) (94), 161 (b) (92), 168 (b) (91), 170 (hg) (94), 170 (hd) (94), 170 (b) (91), 171 (94), 172 (h) (94), 172 (b) (92), 176 (94), 177 (94), 178 (h) (92), 178 (b) (92), 180 (h) (92), 181 (92), 183 (h) (94), 183 (bd) (92). **Kenney Bassett** : pp. 118 (b) (85), 175 (h) (85). **William Borel** : p. 8 (94). **Jean-Paul Caron** : pp. 67 (h), 163 (b) (94). **Marc Tienda** : p. 164 (h) (94). **Eric Vargiolu** : pp. 11 (hd), 79 (94), 146 (b) (94).

Illustrations
Fernand Forest : pp. 10 (m), 10 (g), 10 (b), 11 (h), 14 (h). **Collection Yachting Heritage** : p.26. **Collection privée** : pp. 66, 71, 188, 189. **Keystone-l'Illustration** : p. 91.

Index